ASSESSMENT OF CHILDREN
Revised and Updated Third Edition
WAIS–III SUPPLEMENT

Jerome M. Sattler

San Diego State University

and

Joseph J. Ryan

Dwight D. Eisenhower Veterans Affairs Medical Center

Jerome M. Sattler, Publisher, Inc.
San Diego, CA

Editorial Services: Sally Lifland and Denise Throckmorton, Lifland et al., Bookmakers
Interior Design: Jerome M. Sattler and Sally Lifland
Cover Designer: Jerome M. Sattler
Production Coordinators: Sally Lifland and Jerome M. Sattler
Cover Printer: Maple-Vail Book Manufacturing Group
Printer and Binder: Maple-Vail Book Manufacturing Group

This text was set in Times and Helvetica and printed on High Bright Vellum.

Cover: Black and white reproduction of Tridem-K by Vasarely ©
S.P.A.D.E.M., Paris/V.A.G.A., New York, 1986.

16 15 14 13 12 11 10 9 8 7 6 5 4 3 2 1   06 05 04 03 02 01 00 99 98

Printed in the United States of America

CONTENTS

List of Tables and Exhibits   v
Preface and Acknowledgments   vii

Appendix N. Wechsler Adult Intelligence Scale–III (WAIS–III)   1203

Standardization   1204
Deviation IQs and Scaled Scores   1205
Reliability   1206
Validity   1210
Intercorrelations Between Subtests
    and Scales   1213
Factor Analyses   1214
Range of Subtest Scores   1220
Range of Full Scale IQs   1220
Comparison of the WAIS–III
    and WAIS–R   1221
Administering the WAIS–III   1222
Short Forms of the WAIS–III   1239
Choosing Between the WAIS–III
    and the WISC–III   1242
WAIS–III Subtests   1243
Interpreting the WAIS–III   1252
Assets of the WAIS–III   1259
Limitations of the WAIS–III   1260
Thinking Through the Issues   1260
Summary   1261

Appendix O. Tables for the WAIS–III   1265

References   1285
Index   1287

LIST OF TABLES AND EXHIBITS

Tables in Appendix N

N-1. Demographic Characteristics of WAIS–III Standardization Sample: Education and Geographic Region by Race/Ethnic Group 1205

N-2. Reliability Coefficients and Standard Errors of Measurement for WAIS–III Subtests, Scales, and Index Scores for 16- to 17-Year-Olds and for the Average of the 13 Age Groups in the Standardization Sample 1207

N-3. Range and Median Internal Consistency Reliabilities of WAIS–III Subtests for 13 Age Groups 1208

N-4. Test-Retest Stability Coefficients of the WAIS–III for Four Age Groups 1208

N-5. Test-Retest WAIS–III IQs for Four Age Groups 1209

N-6. Test-Retest Gains or Losses on the WAIS–III for Four Age Groups 1210

N-7. Chart to Locate Confidence Intervals in Table L-2 (Pages 1137–1148), Based on Estimated True Scores for WAIS–III 1211

N-8. Summary of WAIS–III Criterion-Related Validity Studies Cited in the *WAIS–III—WMS–III Technical Manual* 1213

N-9. Average Correlations Between WAIS–III Subtests and Verbal, Performance, and Full Scales 1214

N-10. Factor Loadings of WAIS–III Subtests for 13 Age Groups and the Average of All Age Groups Following Principal Factor Analysis (Four-Factor Solution, Oblimin Rotation) 1216

N-11. Summary of Principal Factor Analysis on WAIS–III by Age Group and for the Average of the Total Sample 1218

N-12. WAIS–III Subtests as Measures of *g* 1218

N-13. Amount of Specificity in WAIS–III Subtests for 13 Age Groups and the Average of All Age Groups 1219

N-14. Maximum WAIS–III Subtest Scaled Scores by Age Group 1221

N-15. Highlights of Changes in WAIS–III 1223

N-16. Median Number of Digits Recalled on WAIS–III Digits Forward and Digits Backward, by Age Group 1245

N-17. Percentage of Individuals in Standardization Group Who Recalled More WAIS–III Digits Backward Than Digits Forward, by Age Group 1245

N-18. Additional Scaled-Score Points by Age Group Awarded to WAIS–III Subtests When the Reference Group (Ages 20–34 Years) Receives a Scaled Score of 10 1258

Tables in Appendix O

O-1. Confidence Intervals for WAIS–III Scales and Index Scores Based on Obtained Score Only 1266

O-2. Significant Differences Between WAIS–III Scaled Scores, IQs, and Index Scores for Ages 16–17, 18–19, and for the Average of the 13 Age Groups (.05/.01 significance levels) 1269

O-3. Differences Required for Significance When Each WAIS–III Subtest Scaled Score Is Compared to the Mean Subtest Scaled Score for an Individual Examinee 1270

O-4. Estimates of Probability of Obtaining Designated Differences Between Individual WAIS–III Verbal and Performance IQs by Chance 1272

O-5. Estimates of the Probability of Obtaining Designated Differences Between Individual WAIS–III Index Score Deviation Quotients (DQs) by Chance 1273

O-6. Reliability and Validity Coefficients of Proposed WAIS–III Short Forms 1274

O-7. Estimated WAIS–III Full Scale Deviation Quotients for Sum of Scaled Scores for Ten Best Short-Form Dyads and Other Combinations 1275

O-8. Estimated WAIS–III Full Scale Deviation Quotients for Sum of Scaled Scores for Ten Best Short-Form Triads and Other Combinations 1277

O-9. Estimated WAIS–III Full Scale Deviation Quotients for Sum of Scaled Scores for Ten Best Short-Form Tetrads and Other Combinations 1279

O-10. Estimated WAIS–III Full Scale Deviation Quotients for Sum of Scaled Scores for Ten Best Short-Form Pentads and Other Combinations 1281

O-11. Estimated WAIS–III Full Scale Deviation Quotients for Sum of Scaled Scores for One Six-Subtest Short-Form Combination and Two Seven-Subtest Short-Form Combinations 1283

Exhibits in Appendix N

N-1. Supplementary Instructions for Administering the WAIS–III 1226

N-2. Administrative Checklist for the WAIS–III 1228

PREFACE AND ACKNOWLEDGMENTS

Assessment of Children, Revised and Updated Third Edition, WAIS–III Supplement contains two appendixes that accompany the main 1992 text. The supplement must be used in conjunction with the main text, *Assessment of Children, Revised and Updated Third Edition,* to have the full complement of tables and guidelines needed to interpret the WAIS–III.

The *WAIS–III Supplement* follows the format of the main text. Appendix N parallels Chapter 10 on the WAIS–R; Appendix O parallels Appendixes C and L.

References cited in the *WAIS–III Supplement* can be found in the reference section of the supplement.

The WAIS–III is a refinement of a clinical and psychoeducational tool that first appeared in the 1930s. David Wechsler's work is being carried on by the staff of The Psychological Corporation. And, although David Wechsler died in 1981, he is still listed as the author of the revised version of the WAIS–III.

The material in the supplement was written to help readers become master clinicians in administering and interpreting the WAIS–III. Your comments about this work will be most appreciated.

We wish to thank several professionals and students who have graciously given their time to review the supplement. They are as follows:

Dr. Leslie Atkinson, Clarke Institute of Psychiatry
Granville M. "Bow" Bowman, San Diego State University
Dr. Larry Hilgert, Valdosta State College
Dr. William A. Hillix, San Diego State University
Dr. Aurilio Prifitera, The Psychological Corporation
Adria Sandroni, San Diego State University
Bonnie J. Sattler, Kaiser Foundation Health Plan
Dr. David Tulsky, The Psychological Corporation

Dr. Lisa Weyandt, Central Washington University
Darlene Wheeler, University of California, Riverside

We also wish to acknowledge the help of other individuals who contributed to the supplement:

Michael Irwin, from the Test Office at San Diego State University, was of great assistance in writing the computer programs necessary to generate the tables in Appendix O. Thank you, Mike, for your excellent work and kindness. We also wish to thank Anthony M. Paolo for his help with the factor analysis.

Sharon Drum, secretary to Jerome M. Sattler, did an excellent job of typing the tables. Thank you, Sharon. Brenda Piendo, the office manager of Jerome M. Sattler, Publisher, Inc., is to be thanked for her help in getting the book into production.

Roy Wallace, representing Maple-Vail Book Manufacturing Group, has again been excellent to work with. Thank you, Roy, for your help and assistance.

And finally, we wish to thank Sally Lifland and Denise Throckmorton, from Lifland et al., Bookmakers, for doing an excellent job in editing the manuscript. Sally Lifland also coordinated the numerous production details, for which she deserves additional thanks.

June 1998
Jerome M. Sattler
San Diego State University
Psychology Department
San Diego, CA 92182-4611

Joseph J. Ryan
Dwight D. Eisenhower Veterans Affairs
Medical Center
Psychology Service (116B)
Leavenworth, KS 66048

APPENDIX N

WECHSLER ADULT INTELLIGENCE SCALE–III (WAIS–III)

We should take care not to make the intellect our god; it has, of course, powerful muscles, but no personality.

—Albert Einstein

Standardization
Deviation IQs and Scaled Scores
Validity
Intercorrelations Between Subtests and Scales
Factor Analyses
Range of Subtest Scores
Range of Full Scale IQs
Comparison of the WAIS–III and WAIS–R
Administering the WAIS–III
Short Forms of the WAIS–III
Choosing Between the WAIS–III and the
    WISC–III
WAIS–III Subtests
Interpreting the WAIS–III
Assets of the WAIS–III
Limitations of the WAIS–III
Thinking Through the Issues
Summary

The Wechsler Adult Intelligence Scale–III (WAIS–III; Wechsler, 1997) is the latest edition of an intelligence test introduced in 1939. In its original version, it was called the Wechsler-Bellevue Intelligence Scale, Form I (Wechsler, 1939), after David Wechsler and Bellevue Hospital in New York City, where Wechsler served as chief psychologist. Other editions included the Wechsler-Bellevue Intelligence Scale, Form II, published in 1946; the WAIS, published in 1955; and the WAIS–R, published in 1981. The Wechsler Intelligence Scale for Children–III (WISC–III) and the Wechsler Preschool and Primary Scale of Intelligence–Revised (WPPSI–R) also are derivatives of the 1939 adult scale. Because this textbook focuses on testing children, use of the WAIS–III with examinees 16 to 17 years old will be highlighted.

The WAIS–III contains 14 subtests that are grouped according to Verbal and Performance Scales. The six standard subtests within the Verbal Scale are Vocabulary, Similarities, Arithmetic, Digit Span, Information, and Comprehension. The five standard subtests within the Performance Scale are Picture Completion, Digit Symbol—Coding, Block Design, Matrix Reasoning, and Picture Arrangement. The three remaining subtests are Letter–Number Sequencing in the Verbal Scale and Symbol Search and Object Assembly in the Performance Scale. Letter–Number Sequencing and Symbol Search are designated as supplementary subtests because they contribute only to Index scores; these are essentially factor scores, which are discussed later in this appendix. Object Assembly is designated as an optional subtest because it is not included in any Index score, but it can provide useful clinical information about perceptual organization.

Although numerous modifications have been made in the third edition, the basic structure of the WAIS–III is the same as that of the WAIS–R. More than 68 percent (113) of the 165 WAIS–R items (excluding Digit Symbol—Coding) are retained in the WAIS–III, in either the original or modified form. One of the primary differences between the WAIS–R and the WAIS–III is that the revision covers a broader age range. The 16 years 0 months to 74 years 11 months WAIS–R age range has been extended to an age range of 16 years 0 months to 89 years 11 months for the WAIS–III.

STANDARDIZATION

The WAIS–III was standardized on 2,450 individuals selected to be representative of the late-adolescent and adult population in the United States during the early to mid 1990s. The demographic characteristics used to obtain a stratified sample were age, sex, race/ethnicity, educational level, and geographic region.

In the standardization sample, there were 13 age groups: 16–17, 18–19, 20–24, 25–29, 30–34, 35–44, 45–54, 55–64, 65–69, 70–74, 75–79, 80–84, and 85–89 years. In each age group between 16 and 64 years, there were 100 males and 100 females. In the age groups from 65 to 89 years, there were more women than men, in proportions consistent with the U.S. census data (i.e., 65–69 years: 90 males and 110 females; 70–74 years: 88 males and 112 females; 75–79 years: 83 males and 117 females; 80–84 years: 54 males and 96 females; 85–89 years: 32 males and 68 females).

For race/ethnicity membership, individuals were classified as White ($N = 1,925$), African American ($N = 279$), Hispanic ($N = 181$), and Other ($N = 65$).

The five educational categories ranged from less than or equal to 8 years of education to greater than or equal to 16 years of education. For individuals in the age range 16 to 19 years, parental education, rather than the individuals' educational levels, was used to stratify the samples.

The four geographic regions sampled were Northeast, North Central, South, and West. Table N-1 shows the educational status and geographic location by race/ethnicity of the standardization sample.

The WAIS–III was co-normed with the Wechsler Memory Scale–III (WMS–III; Wechsler, 1997) with a sample of individuals 16 to 89 years old ($N = 1,250$). In addition, a sample of individuals 16 to 19 years old ($N = 142$) was given both the WAIS–III and the Wechsler Individual Achievement Test (WIAT; Wechsler, 1991). This sample was referred to as a "linking sample" in the *WAIS–III Technical Manual*. Conorming of the WAIS–III and Wechsler Memory Scale–III will assist you in evaluating an examinee's memory functions in relation to her or his level of intellectual functioning. Similarly, linking the WAIS–III and WIAT will help you in evaluating an examinee's achievement

Table N-1
Demographic Characteristics of WAIS–III Standardization Sample: Education and Geographic Region by Race/Ethnic Group

Demographic variable	Race/ethnic group (percent)			
	White	Black	Hispanic	Other
Amount of education				
≤ 8 years	9.8	13.3	29.8	6.2
9–11 years	10.3	17.2	18.2	13.8
12 years	36.1	34.4	25.4	24.6
13–15 years	23.8	23.3	19.3	32.3
≥ 16 years	19.9	11.8	7.2	23.1
Total	99.9	100.0	99.9	100.0
Geographic region				
Northeast	19.2	16.5	7.7	16.9
North Central	26.4	30.8	7.7	24.5
South	32.4	37.3	66.9	35.4
West	21.9	15.4	17.7	23.1
Total	99.9	100.0	100.0	100.1

Note. Race/ethnic distribution in the total group was as follows: White, 78.6%; Black, 11.4%; Hispanic, 7.4%; Other, 2.6%.
Source: Adapted from The Psychological Corporation (1997).

level in relation to his or her level of intellectual functioning.

DEVIATION IQs AND SCALED SCORES

The WAIS–III, like the WISC–III and WPPSI–R, uses the Deviation IQ (M = 100, SD = 15) for each of the Verbal, Performance, and Full Scales, and standard scores (M = 10, SD = 3) for each of the 14 individual subtests. An IQ is computed by comparing the examinee's scores with the scores earned by a representative sample of his or her age group. After each subtest is scored, raw point totals are converted to scaled scores within the examinee's own age group through use of Table A.1 in the *WAIS–III Administration and Scoring Manual* (Wechsler, 1997; pp. 181–194). Age groups are 2-year intervals for individuals 16 to 19 years, 10-year intervals for persons between 35 and 64 years, and 5-year intervals for individuals in the age ranges 20 to 34 years and 65 to 89 years.

The table in the *WAIS–III Administration and Scoring Manual* used to obtain IQs (Table A.3, pp. 195–198) is based on the 11 standard subtests. The two supplementary subtests, Letter–Number Sequencing and Symbol Search, are not used in the calculation of IQs unless the former replaces Digit Span and the latter replaces Digit Symbol—Coding. The optional subtest, Object Assembly, also is not used in the calculation of IQs unless it is substituted for a Performance Scale subtest. When a supplementary or optional subtest is substituted for a standard subtest, little is known about the exact reliability and validity of the IQs because the supplementary and optional subtests were not used in the construction of the tables used to generate IQs. Moreover, the Letter–Number Sequencing subtest was not administered to the entire standardization sample—only to the 1,250 individuals who also completed the WMS–III. According to the *WAIS–III Administration and Scoring Manual* (p. 54), however, a series of statistical analyses using the normative sample demonstrated that Object Assembly may replace Matrix Reasoning in the determination of the Performance and Full Scale IQs without affecting scores. No statistical analyses were provided to support this statement, however. Also note that because Object Assembly has a lower reliability than Matrix Reasoning (r_{xx} = .70 vs. r_{xx} = .90), the Performance IQ and Full Scale IQ reliabilities are likely to be lower when Object Assembly is substituted for Matrix Reasoning.

The two WAIS–III manuals (*WAIS–III Administration and Scoring Manual* and *WAIS–III—WMS–III Technical Manual*) provide guidelines for use of the supplementary and optional subtests. These instructions, in part, indicate that Letter–Number Sequencing may substitute only for Digit Span in determining the Verbal IQ, and Symbol Search may replace only Digit Symbol—Coding in calculating the Performance IQ. These substitutions are permitted only when one or both of the designated subtests have been spoiled. The optional subtest, Object Assembly, may be substituted for any spoiled Performance subtest when the examinee is in the age range 16 to 74 years. Unfortunately, the two WAIS–III manuals fail to discuss how these recommendations were reached. It would have been helpful to practitioners if The Psychological Corporation had cited research findings to support its recommendations. It would appear reasonable to substitute any subtests as needed because all of the subtests have adequate reliability. In addition, it is likely that the IQs computed with Letter–Number Sequencing, Symbol Search, and Object Assembly will be reliable and valid. However, research studies are needed to determine what actual effects, if any, subtest substitutions have on the obtained IQs.

Scaled Scores

The *WAIS–III Administration and Scoring Manual* provides two tables for determining subtest scaled scores. The principal one is Table A.1, on page 181. This table is used in converting raw scores to scaled scores relative to the examinee's own age group. The second one is Table A.2, on page 194, which provides supplemental norms. This table is based on a census-matched reference group of persons ranging from 20 to 34 years of age ($N = 600$). *The subtest scaled scores in Table A.2 are not age-corrected and should never be used for the computation of IQs or Index scores.* The scores in Table A.2, however, can be used when you want to compare an older examinee's scaled scores with those of a young-adult group.

Prorating Procedure

The *WAIS–III Administration and Scoring Manual* provides Table A.10, on page 203, for prorating sums of scaled scores when you administer only five Verbal Scale subtests and four Performance Scale subtests. Tellegen and Briggs (1967) provide another procedure (see page 138 in the text) for computing IQs obtained on an abbreviated version of the test (also referred to as a short form). Their procedure considers the intercorrelations between the specific subtests administered; prorating does not take the intercorrelations into account. Later in this appendix we discuss how you can obtain estimated IQs for several short-form subtest combinations using the Tellegen and Briggs procedure. We need research to determine which procedure—prorating or the Tellegen and Briggs procedure—produces more valid IQs.

RELIABILITY

The WAIS–III has excellent reliability. The three scales have internal consistency reliability coefficients of .93 or above over the entire age range covered in the standardization sample.

Average internal consistency reliability coefficients, based on the 13 age groups, are .98 for the Full Scale IQ, .97 for the Verbal Scale IQ, and .94 for the Performance Scale IQ (see Table N-2). The reliability coefficients for ages 16 to 89 years range from .97 to .98 for the Full Scale IQ, .96 to .98 for the Verbal Scale IQ, and .93 to .96 for the Performance Scale IQ.

Subtest Reliabilities

The internal consistency reliabilities for the subtests are lower than those for the three scales, as would be expected. The average internal consistency reliabilities range from a low of .70 for Object Assembly to a high of .93 for Vocabulary (see Table N-2). For the 13 age groups, median subtest reliabilities range from a low of .83 at two age groups to a high of .87 at four age groups (see Table N-3). Thus, there are no distinct differences in subtest internal consistency reliabilities as a function of age.

The highest reliabilities are found among the six standard Verbal subtests (average reliabilities range from .84 to .93). Vocabulary ($r_{xx} = .93$) is the most reliable Verbal Scale subtest. Average reliabilities among the five standard Performance Scale subtests range from .74 to .90. Matrix Reasoning is the most reliable Performance Scale subtest ($r_{xx} = .90$). Reliability coefficients for 10 of the 11 standard subtests, and for Letter–Number Sequencing and Object Assembly, are split-half correlations corrected by the Spearman-Brown formula. For Digit Symbol—Coding and Symbol Search, the reliability estimates are test-retest stability coefficients because the items comprising these subtests do not lend themselves to the split-half calculation procedure.

Standard Errors of Measurement

The average standard errors of measurement (SE_m) in IQ points are 2.30 for the Full Scale, 2.55 for the Verbal Scale, and 3.67 for the Performance Scale (see Table N-2). Thus, as with all Wechsler scales, you can place more confidence in IQs based on the Full Scale than in those based on either the Verbal Scale or the Performance Scale. In addition, you can place more confidence in IQs obtained from the Verbal Scale than in those obtained from the Performance Scale. Across the 13 age groups, the

Table N-2
Reliability Coefficients and Standard Errors of Measurement for WAIS–III Subtests, Scales, and Index Scores for 16- to 17-Year-Olds and for the Average of the 13 Age Groups in the Standardization Sample

Subtest, Scale, or Index	Reliability coefficient		Standard error of measurement	
	16- to 17-year-olds	Average of standardization group	16- to 17-year-olds	Average of standardization group
Vocabulary	.90	.93	.95	.79
Similarities	.81	.86	1.31	1.12
Arithmetic	.88	.88	1.04	1.05
Digit Span	.90	.90	.95	.94
Information	.89	.91	.99	.91
Comprehension	.84	.84	1.20	1.21
Letter–Number Sequencing	.77	.82	1.44	1.30
Picture Completion	.82	.83	1.27	1.25
Digit Symbol—Coding	.81	.84	1.31	1.19
Block Design	.88	.86	1.04	1.14
Matrix Reasoning	.87	.90	1.08	.97
Picture Arrangement	.70	.74	1.64	1.53
Symbol Search	.74	.77	1.53	1.43
Object Assembly	.73	.70	1.56	1.66
Verbal Scale IQ	.96	.97	2.87	2.55
Performance Scale IQ	.93	.94	4.03	3.67
Full Scale IQ	.97	.98	2.58	2.30
Verbal Comprehension	.94	.96	3.61	3.01
Perceptual Organization	.93	.93	4.03	3.95
Working Memory	.93	.94	3.98	3.84
Processing Speed	.86	.88	5.56	5.13

Note. Reliabilities for Digit Symbol—Coding and Symbol Search are test-retest stability coefficients. Reliabilities for the other 12 subtests are split-half correlations.
Source: Technical Manual of the Wechsler Adult Intelligence Scale: Third Edition/Wechsler Memory Scale: Third Edition. Copyright © 1997 by The Psychological Corporation. Reproduced by permission. All rights reserved. "Wechsler Adult Intelligence Scale," "Wechsler Memory Scale," and "WMS" are registered trademarks of The Psychological Corporation.

standard errors of measurement for the subtests in scaled-score points range from .67 (at 65–69 years) to 1.50 (at 35–44 years and 75–79 years) for the Verbal Scale subtests and from .73 (at 65–69 years) to 2.12 (at 85–89 years) for the Performance Scale subtests. Within the Verbal Scale, Vocabulary has the smallest average SE_m (.79) and Letter–Number Sequencing has the largest average SE_m (1.30). Among the six standard Verbal Scale subtests, Comprehension has the highest SE_m (1.21). Within the Performance Scale, Matrix Reasoning has the smallest average SE_m (.97) and Object Assembly has the largest average SE_m (1.66). Among the five standard Performance Scale subtests, Picture Arrangement has the largest average SE_m (1.53).

Test-Retest Stability

In the standardization sample, the stability of the WAIS–III was assessed by having 394 individuals from the 13 age groups (approximately 30 individuals from each group) retested after an interval ranging from 14 to 84 days (M = 34.6 days; Wechsler, 1997). For statistical analyses, individuals were then combined into four age groups (16–29 years, 30–54 years, 55–74 years, and 75–89 years). In the four age groups, the uncorrected stability coefficients were, respectively, .91, .96, .96, and .96 for the Full Scale IQ; .91, .95, .97, and .94 for the Verbal Scale IQ; and .83, .88, .91, and .93 for the Performance Scale IQ. Thus, the WAIS–III provides

Table N-3
Range and Median Internal Consistency Reliabilities of WAIS–III Subtests for 13 Age Groups

Age group	Range r_{xx}	Median r_{xx}
16–17	.70–.90	.83
18–19	.70–.93	.87
20–24	.70–.94	.84
25–29	.71–.92	.86
30–34	.66–.94	.86
35–44	.71–.93	.86
45–54	.75–.92	.86
55–64	.72–.94	.88
65–69	.77–.95	.87
70–74	.68–.93	.87
75–79	.59–.93	.84
80–84	.64–.94	.87
85–89	.50–.93	.83
Average	.70–.93	.85

Source: Adapted from The Psychological Corporation (1997).

Table N-4
Test-Retest Stability Coefficients of the WAIS–III for Four Age Groups

Subtest, Scale, or Index	Age group (in years)				
	16–29	30–54	55–74	75–89	Av.[a]
Vocabulary	.85	.93	.92	.79	.91
Similarities	.73	.85	.84	.82	.83
Arithmetic	.80	.87	.86	.83	.86
Digit Span	.75	.79	.85	.69	.83
Information	.92	.93	.93	.94	.94
Comprehension	.67	.80	.83	.75	.81
Letter–Number Seq.	.48	.74	.77	.71	.75
Picture Completion	.66	.79	.82	.82	.79
Digit Symbol—Coding	.80	.84	.85	.91	.86
Block Design	.77	.86	.77	.76	.82
Matrix Reasoning	.70	.69	.78	.72	.77
Picture Arrangement	.60	.70	.62	.71	.69
Symbol Search	.69	.80	.77	.80	.79
Object Assembly	.64	.78	.76	.65	.76
Verbal Scale IQ	.91	.95	.97	.94	.96
Performance Scale IQ	.83	.88	.91	.93	.91
Full Scale IQ	.91	.96	.96	.96	.96
Verbal Comprehension	.89	.95	.96	.93	.95
Perceptual Organization	.79	.86	.89	.89	.88
Working Memory	.82	.90	.90	.85	.89
Processing Speed	.83	.87	.89	.92	.89

[a] Av. = Average.
Source: Technical Manual of the Wechsler Adult Intelligence Scale: Third Edition/Wechsler Memory Scale: Third Edition. Copyright © 1997 by The Psychological Corporation. Reproduced by permission. All rights reserved. "Wechsler Adult Intelligence Scale," "Wechsler Memory Scale," and "WMS" are registered trademarks of The Psychological Corporation.

stable IQs for the Full Scale, Verbal Scale, and Performance Scale (see Table N-4).

The stability coefficients for the subtests ranged from a low of .48 for Letter–Number Sequencing at 16–29 years to a high of .94 for Information at 75–89 years (see Table N-4). Average test-retest reliabilities for the subtests ranged from .69 for Picture Arrangement to .94 for Information (see Table N-4). Average internal consistency reliabilities are somewhat higher than average test-retest reliabilities ($M\ r_{xx}$ = .84 versus $M\ r_{xx}$ = .78).

Two reasons help to explain why the test-retest stability of the Performance Scale is lower than the test-retest stability of the Verbal Scale. First, the lower reliability of the Performance Scale subtests renders them more vulnerable than subtests on the Verbal Scale to practice effects. Second, retest reliability is limited by internal reliability. Because the Performance subtests have lower internal reliability than the Verbal subtests, we would expect lower retest reliability for the Performance subtests.

Changes in IQs. Table N-5 shows the mean test-retest IQs and standard deviations for the Verbal, Performance, and Full Scales for the four age groups. On average, from the first to the second testing, the Full Scale IQ increased by 3.2 to 5.7 points, the Verbal Scale IQ increased by 2.0 to 3.2 points, and the Performance Scale

IQ increased by 3.7 to 8.3 points. These statistically significant increases, which likely result from practice effects, are greater for the Performance Scale than for the Verbal Scale. In addition, as Table N-5 indicates, there was a trend for retest IQ gains on the Full Scale and Performance Scale to diminish with age. Studies with the WAIS–R also showed that retest gains decreased with age (Ryan, Paolo, & Brungardt, 1992; Wechsler, 1981). Perhaps the smaller practice effects with age indicate an age-related drop in incidental learning, a component of fluid intelligence.

Studies are needed to evaluate the stability of the WAIS–III with other samples, including adolescents and adults, and over longer periods of time. Such research would be helpful in learning about how IQs on the WAIS–III change

Table N-5
Test-Retest WAIS–III IQs for Four Age Groups

| Age group | Scale | First testing | | Second testing | | Change |
		Mean IQ	SD	Mean IQ	SD	
16–29	Verbal	101.4	11.9	104.6	12.6	+3.2*
(N = 100)	Performance	101.6	12.2	109.8	12.7	+8.2*
	Full	101.7	11.7	107.4	12.4	+5.7*
30–54	Verbal	99.3	14.4	101.3	14.9	+2.0*
(N = 102)	Performance	99.9	13.8	108.2	16.6	+8.3*
	Full	99.6	14.3	104.7	15.7	+5.1*
55–74	Verbal	99.0	14.1	101.1	14.2	+2.1*
(N = 104)	Performance	99.1	14.2	104.8	15.7	+5.7*
	Full	99.0	14.3	102.9	15.0	+3.9*
75–89	Verbal	98.9	13.0	101.3	14.7	+2.4*
(N = 88)	Performance	99.4	15.2	103.1	18.7	+3.7*
	Full	99.0	14.1	102.2	16.3	+3.2*

*$p < .001$.
Source: Technical Manual of the Wechsler Adult Intelligence Scale: Third Edition/Wechsler Memory Scale: Third Edition. Copyright © 1997 by The Psychological Corporation. Reproduced by permission. All rights reserved. "Wechsler Adult Intelligence Scale," "Wechsler Memory Scale," and "WMS" are registered trademarks of the Psychological Corporation.

over time in different populations and in different age groups. Although, in general, stability coefficients are high for the WAIS–III, there is no way of knowing precisely the stability of scores for any individual examinee. This is true for all tests—it is not unique to the WAIS–III.

Changes in subtest scores. Table N-6 shows the changes in subtest scaled scores from the first to the second administration. The largest changes were for Picture Completion (increases of .9 to 2.4 scaled-score points), whereas the smallest changes were for Matrix Reasoning (decrease of .1 to an increase of .3). The changes were significantly greater than chance in 36 of the 56 t tests that we conducted. It is difficult to know why the Picture Completion subtest showed the largest retest gains.

Knowing the relationship between subtest gain scores and the internal consistency reliabilities of the subtests is helpful in evaluating the gain scores. Calculation of the Spearman rank-order correlations between the magnitude of gain from test to retest and the reliability of the subtests yielded correlations of –.56, –.63, –.52, and –.57 in the age groups 16–29, 30–54, 55–74, and 75–89 years, respectively. These coefficients are significant at $p < .05$ using a

one-tailed test, suggesting that practice effects are likely to be smaller for the most reliable subtests.

Changes in Index scores. Table N-6 shows the changes in Index scaled scores from the first to the second administration. The largest changes were for Perceptual Organization (increases of 2.7 to 7.4 points), whereas the smallest changes were for Working Memory (increases of 1.3 to 3.1 points). Although the oldest age group (75–89 years) had smaller gains on retest than the other age groups for Perceptual Organization, Working Memory, and Processing Speed, it had the largest gain of the four age groups on Verbal Comprehension. Overall, regardless of age, all groups showed significant gains on retest, with the exception of the 75–89-year age group on Working Memory and Processing Speed, where the increases were not statistically significant.

Confidence Intervals

This text presents tables for two types of confidence intervals. The first is Table O-1 in Appendix O, which is based on the obtained score

Table N-6
Test-Retest Gains or Losses on the WAIS–III for Four Age Groups

Subtest or Index	Age group			
	16–29	30–54	55–74	75–89
Vocabulary	0.2	0.1	0.2	0.4*
Similarities	0.6**	0.3	0.4*	0.7***
Arithmetic	0.6***	0.3	0.3	0.5**
Digit Span	0.5*	0.4*	0.4**	−0.1
Information	0.6***	0.6***	0.5***	0.6***
Comprehension	0.4*	0.1	0.1	0.3
Letter–Number Sequencing	0.1	0.7**	0.3	0.5
Picture Completion	2.3***	2.4***	1.6***	0.9***
Digit Symbol—Coding	1.2***	1.1***	0.8***	0.6***
Block Design	1.0***	0.7***	0.2	0.3
Matrix Reasoning	0.1	0.3	0.2	−0.1
Picture Arrangement	1.2***	1.2***	1.2**	0.7**
Symbol Search	1.0***	0.5**	0.5*	−0.2
Object Assembly	2.3***	1.6***	1.0***	0.9**
Verbal Comprehension	2.5***	2.1***	1.9***	3.2***
Perceptual Organization	7.3***	7.4***	4.0***	2.7**
Working Memory	2.9**	3.1***	2.2***	1.3
Processing Speed	6.0***	4.6***	3.8***	1.3

*$p < .05$.
**$p < .01$.
***$p < .001$.
Source: Adapted from The Psychological Corporation (1997).

and the standard error of measurement (SE_m). The second is Table L-2 in Appendix L (pages 1139–1148), which uses the estimated true score and the standard error of estimation (SE_E). The *WAIS–III Administration and Scoring Manual* (Tables A.3–A.9), in contrast, provides confidence intervals based on the estimated true score only and for the total group only. The procedures discussed in Appendix I (pages 1037–1040) concerning proper utilization of the SE_m and the SE_E apply to the WAIS–III and to all tests. We recommend that you use Table O-1 in Appendix O to obtain the confidence intervals for individual test administrations.

Table O-1 in Appendix O shows the 68, 85, 90, 95, and 99 percent confidence intervals based on the obtained score and the SE_m for the 13 age groups and the total standardization sample. In contrast, Table L-2 in Appendix L (pages 1137–1148) shows the 68, 85, 90, 95, and 99 percent confidence intervals based on the estimated true score and the SE_E. If you need to use Table L-2 in Appendix L for any purpose, you will need to know the reliability coefficient for each WAIS–III scale in each age group. Table N-7 shows the specific part of Table L-2 that

you should use for each age and scale. The confidence intervals in this text are more appropriate than the ones in the *WAIS–III Administration and Scoring Manual* because they are based on the examinee's specific age.

VALIDITY

Because the WAIS–III is a newly published test, relatively little is known about its validity. Approximately 70 percent of the items on the WAIS–III are from the WAIS–R, and approximately 30 percent are new. It seems plausible, therefore, that research concerning the validity of the WAIS–R applies to the WAIS–III. Studies related to the validity of the WAIS–R, reviewed in Chapter 10 (pages 223–227), indicate that the WAIS–R had adequate concurrent and construct validity for many different types of normal and clinical samples in the age range 16 to 74 years. In addition, the *WAIS–III—WMS–III Technical Manual* (The Psychological Corporation, 1997) presents studies that focus on the content, concurrent, and construct validity of the WAIS–III. These studies are summarized below.

**Table N-7
Chart to Locate Confidence Intervals in
Table L-2 (Pages 1137–1148), Based on
Estimated True Scores for WAIS–III**

	WAIS–III		
Age group	Verbal Scale	Performance Scale	Full Scale
16–17	L	I	M
18–19	M	I	M
20–24	M	I	N
25–29	M	K	N
30–34	M	I	N
35–44	M	J	N
45–54	M	J	N
55–64	N	K	N
65–69	N	L	N
70–74	M	K	N
75–79	M	I	M
80–84	M	J	N
85–89	L	J	M
Average	M	J	N

Content Validity

The degree to which test items are representative of the defined construct or domain under study provides evidence of content validity. Expert professional judgment plays an integral part in determining content validity. Three primary steps were taken to ensure adequate content validity of the WAIS–III: (a) comprehensive literature reviews were completed to identify problematic items within the WAIS–R; (b) items from the WAIS–R, along with suggested new items provided by psychologists, were scrutinized by consultants for content coverage and relevance, as well as for possible revision or deletion; and (c) surveys and focus groups composed of clinical practitioners and assessment professionals were used to further evaluate item content, usefulness, and relevance. Finally, an advisory panel of psychologists and researchers reviewed and critiqued the results of steps a, b, and c. The panel also made recommendations concerning the development of new subtests, improvement of existing subtests, development of summary scores, and selection of individual test items (The Psychological Corporation, 1997).

Concurrent Validity

The degree to which a test is related to an established criterion measure, when both instruments are administered at approximately the same time, reflects concurrent validity. The *WAIS–III—WMS–III Technical Manual* reports the findings of a series of studies in which the WAIS–III was given along with the WAIS–R, WISC–III, Stanford-Binet: Fourth Edition, Standard Progressive Matrices, and measures of memory and academic achievement. Let's review these findings.

WAIS–III and WAIS–R. A sample of 192 persons between 16 and 74 years of age was administered the WAIS–III and WAIS–R in counterbalanced order within a 2- to 12-week period (The Psychological Corporation, 1997). The median retest interval was 4.7 weeks. The group was predominantly Caucasian (i.e., 79.2 percent White, 11.5 percent Black, 6.8 percent Hispanic, 2.5 percent other) and composed of approximately equal numbers of men and women (48.4 percent males, 51.6 percent females). The correlations between the tests were .94 for the Verbal Scale, .86 for the Performance Scale, and .93 for the Full Scale. For the 11 subtests that appear on both versions of the test, correlations ranged from a low of .50 for Picture Completion to a high of .90 for Vocabulary (*Mdn r* = .77). Subtests on the Verbal Scale have higher correlations (range of .76 to .90, *Mdn r* = .81) than do those on the Performance Scale (range of .50 to .77, *Mdn r* = .69). The high correlations are not surprising because most items are the same in both tests. What is less clear is why the correlations are relatively low for some of the Performance Scale subtests, particularly Picture Completion.

The low correlation on Picture Completion may have resulted from the fact that Picture Completion was the most substantially modified subtest in the revision. Only 40 percent of the WAIS–R Picture Completion items were retained in the WAIS–III, and all items on the WAIS–III subtest were enlarged and colored.

For the Verbal, Performance, and Full Scales, mean IQs were *lower* on the WAIS–III than on the WAIS–R. The average difference was 1.2 points on the Verbal Scale (102.2 vs. 103.4), 4.8 points on the Performance Scale (103.5 vs. 108.3), and 2.9 points on the Full Scale (102.9 vs. 105.8). These results are consistent with previous findings that individuals tend to score lower on new tests than on older ones (Flynn, 1984, 1987).

The relationship between the WAIS–R and the WAIS–III needs further investigation. For example, because the individuals used to compare the WAIS–R and the WAIS–III were all younger than 75 years old and generally of average ability, we have no way of knowing whether the two tests produce comparable IQs at other ages and ability levels. Until additional research becomes available, you need to be cautious when interpreting results for individuals tested with the WAIS–R and then with the WAIS–III. However, preliminary research suggests that individuals with average ability who are between 16 and 74 years of age will likely obtain somewhat lower scores on the WAIS–III than on the WAIS–R.

As noted in Appendix I, when a counterbalanced design is used to evaluate changes from one Wechsler Scale to another (i.e., one group is given first one test and then the other test, and then the order of the two tests is switched when the tests are given to another group), the scores on the second test are confounded by practice effects. In a counterbalanced design, performance on the second test administered is likely to be influenced by prior exposure to the first test. This is even more likely to happen when there are overlapping items on the two tests. Thus, the results for the second test are not clean; only the results for the first test are uncontaminated. In order to ascertain whether scores on two tests differ, we need to have data from independent test administrations. In the study reported in the *WAIS–III—WMS–III Technical Manual* in which the WAIS–III and the WAIS–R were counterbalanced, the independent test data would be from the first administration of each test only. Unfortunately, these data were not provided by the test publisher. Practice effects have probably made the means in the tables a bit high.

WAIS–III and WISC–III. Because the WAIS–III and WISC–III overlap at ages 16 to 17 years, it is important to have information about the relationship between the two tests for this age group. The WAIS–III and WISC–III were administered in counterbalanced order to a sample of 184 16-year-olds (The Psychological Corporation, 1997). The interval between the two test administrations ranged from 2 to 12 weeks (*Mdn* = 4.6 weeks). The correlations were .88 for the Verbal Scale, .78 for the Performance Scale, and .88 for the Full Scale.

For the 11 subtests that the WAIS–III and WISC–III have in common, correlations ranged from a low of .31 for Picture Arrangement to a high of .83 for Vocabulary (*Mdn r* = .73). Subtests on the Verbal Scale have higher correlations (range of .60 to .83, *Mdn r* = .74) than do those on the Performance Scale (range of .31 to .80, *Mdn r* = .64).

For the Verbal, Performance, and Full Scales, mean IQs were slightly higher on the WAIS–III than on the WISC–III. The average difference was .5 point on the Verbal Scale (103.5 vs. 103.0), .4 point on the Performance Scale (104.9 vs. 104.5), and .7 point on the Full Scale (104.6 vs. 103.9). These results suggest that the two scales yield comparable IQs. However, these findings are based on a relatively small sample with predominantly average ability and should not be generalized to individuals at the relative extremes of the intelligence distribution.

Research is needed on the comparability of the WAIS–III and WISC–III in clinical populations, in gifted populations, and in mentally retarded populations. In addition, because the results reported previously were based on a counterbalanced design (i.e., giving the WAIS–III followed by the WISC–III to half the sample and the WISC–III followed by the WAIS–III to the other half of the sample), the scores on the second test administered are affected by practice effects. To examine further the comparability of the WAIS–III and WISC–III, we need results from independent administrations of the two tests to random samples and results from different groups of exceptional adolescents.

WAIS–III and Stanford-Binet: Fourth Edition. Twenty-six normal individuals (*M* age = 28.5) were administered both the WAIS–III and the Stanford-Binet: Fourth Edition (Thorndike, Hagan, & Sattler, 1986) within an unspecified time frame. The mean scores were highly similar. On the Stanford-Binet: Fourth Edition, the mean Composite Score was 114.8 (*SD* = 12.1), and on the WAIS–III, the mean Full Scale IQ was 113.3 (*SD* = 12.2). Correlations between the Stanford-Binet and WAIS–III were .78 for the Verbal IQ, .89 for the Performance IQ, and .88 for the Full Scale IQ.

Table N-8
Summary of WAIS–III Criterion-Related Validity Studies Cited in the *WAIS–III—WMS–III Technical Manual*

Criterion	WAIS–III		
	VS IQ	PS IQ	FS IQ
Wechsler Adult Intelligence Scale–Revised	.94	.86	.93
Wechsler Intelligence Scale for Children–III	.88	.78	.88
Stanford-Binet Intelligence Scale: Fourth Edition	.78	.89	.88
Standard Progressive Matrices	.49	.79	.64
Wechsler Individual Achievement Test			
Reading Composite	.79	.61	.76
Math Composite	.81	.69	.81
Language Composite	.70	.53	.68
Writing Composite	.69	.55	.68
Wechsler Memory Scale–III			
Immediate Memory Composite	.53	.54	.57
General Memory Composite	.56	.56	.60
Working Memory Composite	.62	.65	.68

Note. Abbreviations: VS = Verbal Scale, PS = Performance Scale, FS = Full Scale.
Source: Adapted from The Psychological Corporation (1997).

Other concurrent validity studies. Table N-8 summarizes the results of studies reported in the *WAIS–III—WMS–III Technical Manual* in which the WAIS–III was correlated with other tests of cognitive ability, achievement, and memory. Based on the magnitude and pattern of correlations across the different measures, it appears that the WAIS–III has satisfactory concurrent validity. For the most part, the WAIS–III Full Scale correlates more highly with other measures of intelligence (*Mdn r* = .88) than it does with tests of academic achievement (*Mdn r* = .72) and memory (*Mdn r* = .60). We need, however, additional studies using different populations and different ability, achievement, and memory tests.

Construct Validity

One method of assessing construct validity is factor analysis. Factor analysis can be used to determine the structure and components of intelligence as measured by a given test. Our principal axis factor analysis of the WAIS–III standardization sample indicates that all 14 subtests measure general intelligence (*g*) with a moderate or high degree of success. Our results provide support for interpretation of the Verbal and Performance IQs as separate entities and the Full Scale IQ as a global measure of intelligence. For the majority of the age groups, support for the four Index scores also was found (see the section on factor analysis later in this appendix).

The pattern of intercorrelations discussed below provides evidence of convergent and discriminant validity, which are forms of construct validity. Convergent validity is demonstrated when tasks that theoretically tap similar functions correlate more highly with each other than with tasks that theoretically measure different functions. Discriminant validity is demonstrated when tasks that purport to measure different functions yield relatively low or nonsignificant correlations when they are correlated with each other. The pattern of intercorrelations reveals that tasks of similar functions (e.g., Vocabulary and Similarities) correlate more highly with each other than with tasks that measure somewhat different functions (e.g., Digit Span and Block Design).

INTERCORRELATIONS BETWEEN SUBTESTS AND SCALES

Inspection of the intercorrelations between WAIS–III subtests and scales (see Table 4.12, p. 98, *WAIS–III—WMS–III Technical Manual*) indicates that in the total group, correlations between the 14 subtests range from a low of .26 (Object Assembly and Digit Span) to a high of .77 (Vocabulary and Information; *Mdn r* = .48). The seven highest intercorrelations are between Vocabulary and Information (.77), Vocabulary and Similarities (.76), Vocabulary and Comprehension (.75), Information and Similarities (.70), Information and Comprehension (.70), Comprehension and Similarities (.70), and Digit Symbol—Coding and Symbol Search (.65). The seven lowest subtest intercorrelations are between Object Assembly and Digit Span (.26), Object Assembly and Letter–Number Sequencing (.29), Picture Completion and Digit Span (.30), Object Assembly and Digit Symbol—

Coding (.33), Digit Span and Picture Arrangement (.33), Digit Symbol—Coding and Digit Span (.36), and Digit Span and Block Design (.36).

In the total group, the Verbal Scale subtests correlate more highly with each other (*Mdn r* = .57) than do the Performance Scale subtests (*Mdn r* = .49). Average correlations between the Verbal Scale subtests and the Verbal Scale range from .51 to .83 (*Mdn r* = .76); those between the Performance Scale subtests and the Performance Scale range from .50 to .69 (*Mdn r* = .64). Thus, the Verbal Scale subtests have more in common with each other than do the Performance Scale subtests (see Table N-9).

Average correlations between the 14 individual subtests and the Full Scale range from .52 to .80 (*Mdn r* = .66). Vocabulary has the highest correlation with the Full Scale (.80), followed by Information (.76), Similarities (.76), Comprehension (.75), Arithmetic (.72), Matrix Reasoning (.69), Symbol Search (.66), Block Design (.66), Letter–Number Sequencing (.64), Picture Arrangement (.63), Picture Completion (.60), Object Assembly (.59), Digit Symbol—Coding (.53), and Digit Span (.52). Thus, five of the six standard Verbal subtests and one standard Performance subtest (Matrix Reasoning) correlate more highly with the Full Scale than do the other subtests (see Table N-9). Vocabulary has the highest correlation with the Verbal Scale (.83), and Symbol Search has the highest correlation with the Performance Scale (.69). Overall, the Verbal Scale subtests have higher correlations with the Full Scale (*Mdn r* = .75) than do the Performance Scale subtests (*Mdn r* = .63).

FACTOR ANALYSES

Factor Analysis Reported in the *WAIS–III—WMS–III Technical Manual*

The *WAIS–III—WMS–III Technical Manual* reports a series of exploratory factor analyses (principal axis method) of the standardization sample. The 2,450 adolescent and adult individuals were clustered into five age groups (16–19, 20–34, 35–54, 55–74, and 75–89 years), and their scores on 13 of the 14 subtests were analyzed; the Object Assembly subtest was excluded. The results indicated that, for the most

Table N-9
Average Correlations Between WAIS–III Subtests and Verbal, Performance, and Full Scales

Subtest	Verbal Scale	Performance Scale	Full Scale
Vocabulary	.83	.65	.80
Similarities	.77	.65	.76
Arithmetic	.70	.63	.72
Digit Span	.51	.47	.52
Information	.79	.63	.76
Comprehension	.76	.62	.75
Letter–Number Seq.	.62	.57	.64
Picture Completion	.53	.60	.60
Digit Symbol—Coding	.49	.50	.53
Block Design	.59	.66	.66
Matrix Reasoning	.64	.65	.69
Picture Arrangement	.59	.60	.63
Symbol Search	.57	.69	.66
Object Assembly	.50	.64	.59

Source: Technical Manual of the Wechsler Adult Intelligence Scale: Third Edition/Wechsler Memory Scale: Third Edition. Copyright © 1997 by The Psychological Corporation. Reproduced by permission. All rights reserved. "Wechsler Adult Intelligence Scale," "Wechsler Memory Scale," and "WMS" are registered trademarks of The Psychological Corporation.

part, a four-factor model best describes the WAIS–III. These factors are labeled Verbal Comprehension, Perceptual Organization, Working Memory, and Processing Speed. These factor names are used as labels for a postulated unitary ability that attempts to account for the interrelated performance on the subtests that best define each factor.

The term *Verbal Comprehension* reflects a hypothesized verbal-related ability reflected in item content (verbal) and mental processes (comprehension). Acquired verbal-related knowledge and verbal reasoning are likely measured by this factor. This factor is correlated most closely with scores on the Vocabulary, Information, Comprehension, and Similarities subtests.

The term *Perceptual Organization* describes a hypothesized performance-related ability reflected in item content (perceptual) and mental processes (organization). Nonverbal reasoning, attentiveness to detail, and visual-motor integration are likely measured by this factor. This factor is correlated most closely with scores on the Block Design, Matrix Reasoning, Picture Completion, and Picture Arrangement subtests for three of the four age groups. However, a well-defined Perceptual Organization factor does not emerge for persons in the age range 75–89 years (see Table 4.16, p. 108, *WAIS–III—WMS–III Technical Manual*).

The term *Working Memory* reflects a hypothesized memory-related ability involving short-term memory that requires the holding of information "on line" so that manipulations or calculations can be performed (analogous to a mental scratch pad). Short-term memory is likely measured by this factor. This factor is correlated most closely with scores on the Arithmetic, Digit Span, and Letter–Number Sequencing subtests.

The term *Processing Speed* reflects a hypothesized performance-related ability involving perceptual processing and speed as reflected in both mental and psychomotor performance. Quickness in processing visual information is likely measured by this factor. This factor is correlated most closely with scores on the Digit Symbol—Coding and Symbol Search subtests for three of the age groups. However, in the age group 75–89 years, the factor is more complex, with substantial loadings on Block Design, Picture Completion, and Picture Arrangement (see Table 4.21, p. 109, *WAIS–III—WMS–III Technical Manual*).

Factor Analysis Conducted by Ryan and Sattler

To further clarify the underlying structure of the WAIS–III, we conducted a principal axis factor analysis (extraction limited to two iterations) followed by oblimin rotation on the total sample and on each of the 13 age groups. All 14 subtests were included in the analyses, and a four-factor solution was specified. As you can see in Table N-10, a four-factor solution characterizes the WAIS–III, but the subtests that load on each factor vary somewhat with age. For example, for the Verbal Comprehension factor, Vocabulary, Similarities, Information, and Comprehension are present at every age group and in the total group. However, three Performance Scale subtests—Picture Arrangement, Matrix Reasoning, and Picture Completion—also correlate at .30 or above with the Verbal Comprehension factor at one or more ages. Picture Arrangement, in particular, correlates at .30 or above

with Verbal Comprehension at nine age groups and in the total group. Arithmetic also correlates at .30 or above with the Verbal Comprehension factor at eight age groups.

Picture Completion, Block Design, Matrix Reasoning, Picture Arrangement, and Object Assembly load on the Perceptual Organization factor (.30 or above) at eight age groups and in the total group. Only one Verbal subtest—Letter–Number Sequencing—loads (.30 or above) on the Perceptual Organization factor and only at one age group (25–29 years).

Arithmetic, Digit Span, and Letter–Number Sequencing load on the Working Memory factor (.30 or higher) at eight age groups and in the total group. Three Performance subtests—Matrix Reasoning, Picture Arrangement, and Object Assembly—also load on the Working Memory factor at one or more age groups and in the total group.

Digit Symbol—Coding and Symbol Search load on the Processing Speed factor (.30 or higher) at 12 age groups and in the total group. Other subtests that load on the factor (.30 or higher) at one or more age groups include Letter–Number Sequencing, Picture Completion, Digit Span, and Block Design.

There is no easy explanation for this pattern of subtest loadings. It is important to recognize that a Performance subtest like Picture Arrangement may also have a strong verbal processing component. In addition, why some subtests have meaningful loadings on a factor at some ages and not at others cannot be readily explained. It may be due to sampling differences or measurement error or some unknown factor related to developmental trends. Table N-11 summarizes the major trends in the factor analysis by age level.

Later in this appendix you will read about Index scores based on the factor analysis conducted by The Psychological Corporation. Overall, our factor analysis supports the work of The Psychological Corporation, albeit with some discrepancies.

WAIS–III Subtests as Measures of *g*

Examination of the loadings on the first unrotated factor in the principal axis factor analysis allows one to determine the extent to which the WAIS–III subtests measure general intelligence,

Table N-10
Factor Loadings of WAIS–III Subtests for 13 Age Groups and the Average of All Age Groups Following Principal Factor Analysis (Four-Factor Solution, Oblimin Rotation)

Subtest	16–17	18–19	20–24	25–29	30–34	35–44	45–54	55–64	65–69	70–74	75–79	80–84	85–89	Av.[a]
Factor A — Verbal Comprehension														
Vocabulary	87	87	86	95	85	92	81	89	85	77	90	91	77	91
Similarities	63	69	83	83	80	74	67	78	69	79	71	79	59	77
Arithmetic	34	31	28	49	32	15	38	20	33	20	40	58	13	27
Digit Span	–03	–03	05	27	–07	03	11	10	–01	15	29	15	19	01
Information	76	87	84	85	83	76	72	77	86	63	85	92	76	84
Comprehension	79	78	82	82	78	86	84	66	90	69	82	78	80	81
Letter–Number Seq.	05	00	00	19	02	08	–08	10	27	–10	19	12	02	03
Picture Completion	09	05	04	08	10	17	16	17	42	17	12	05	45	12
Digit Symbol—Coding	12	07	02	–02	11	02	–02	–02	03	05	04	04	02	03
Block Design	07	06	–02	–02	07	–08	07	–09	07	–02	–01	22	03	–03
Matrix Reasoning	25	10	11	12	26	11	34	25	17	01	06	41	–01	11
Picture Arrangement	30	38	29	35	43	39	20	49	20	29	21	35	44	31
Symbol Search	–08	00	–01	01	–08	05	05	06	01	10	–13	–06	00	–01
Object Assembly	03	09	08	–03	–01	04	05	14	02	02	02	04	25	03
Factor B — Perceptual Organization														
Vocabulary	–04	–07	–01	–10	00	–06	04	–16	–09	–02	–07	–08	07	–08
Similarities	11	18	–01	03	09	–01	23	11	09	13	14	–02	24	08
Arithmetic	04	19	31	18	–03	25	17	17	23	07	01	–03	25	13
Digit Span	17	13	–02	08	–04	–08	–05	07	07	–05	–04	–15	08	–01
Information	02	–07	–03	–03	–04	02	17	00	–08	08	02	01	–07	–03
Comprehension	00	12	07	08	03	06	–14	10	16	05	14	14	08	06
Letter–Number Seq.	–12	–12	05	32	13	09	10	–09	–18	08	14	16	–08	01
Picture Completion	44	26	45	62	57	47	41	47	37	41	56	73	04	48
Digit Symbol—Coding	–10	–09	08	–10	–08	04	00	–02	05	00	–01	08	17	–04
Block Design	67	79	74	73	54	79	67	65	68	65	66	42	62	70
Matrix Reasoning	45	25	54	53	18	59	45	45	52	45	42	29	62	49
Picture Arrangement	31	07	36	32	49	26	55	33	32	54	32	29	08	35
Symbol Search	23	19	34	16	27	12	12	18	24	08	14	21	26	15
Object Assembly	74	61	79	81	78	74	76	68	60	77	75	65	54	74
Factor C — Working Memory														
Vocabulary	–07	02	09	10	08	–06	05	05	04	16	–06	04	13	02
Similarities	02	04	01	07	00	13	07	00	07	–14	–01	08	–01	–02
Arithmetic	39	29	40	13	56	53	21	56	45	62	40	25	50	50
Digit Span	60	62	75	38	77	62	69	58	71	50	25	62	55	67
Information	02	01	05	06	04	18	09	14	14	24	06	–11	10	06
Comprehension	07	–07	–09	–07	00	–08	01	18	–08	09	01	–04	11	00
Letter–Number Seq.	86	92	79	37	67	72	73	61	40	63	06	73	71	61
Picture Completion	09	14	11	–07	17	–09	06	05	–12	–06	–15	25	–11	–02
Digit Symbol—Coding	06	04	04	01	02	06	05	01	04	02	–10	64	29	04
Block Design	26	08	19	22	15	12	09	25	14	11	16	11	09	18
Matrix Reasoning	18	51	21	23	46	24	02	24	30	47	29	12	14	33
Picture Arrangement	–03	38	–06	–04	–06	20	–13	–07	03	05	03	18	00	01
Symbol Search	06	01	02	–03	07	08	04	06	12	09	12	72	14	06
Object Assembly	–17	–02	–10	–06	00	–12	09	–13	–03	–05	–08	–08	–31	–10

(Continued)

Table N-10 (Continued)

Subtest	Age group													
	16–17	18–19	20–24	25–29	30–34	35–44	45–54	55–64	65–69	70–74	75–79	80–84	85–89	Av.[a]
	Factor D — Processing Speed													
Vocabulary	13	10	–01	00	03	14	01	13	15	06	08	08	–06	06
Similarities	01	–01	04	01	–01	04	–08	00	12	11	14	10	09	03
Arithmetic	18	18	00	16	09	03	13	01	02	05	11	02	06	00
Digit Span	09	08	12	16	05	16	–03	03	05	01	37	–11	–08	05
Information	06	03	01	–03	07	–08	–09	–01	–04	01	–01	–10	20	–02
Comprehension	–08	02	01	01	07	00	17	–01	–08	11	–13	–08	–17	–03
Letter–Number Seq.	04	05	00	12	02	02	13	24	35	26	44	–28	17	16
Picture Completion	16	19	17	02	–03	18	17	15	19	30	15	–20	41	19
Digit Symbol—Coding	70	76	75	85	64	67	79	82	74	66	80	25	57	73
Block Design	–04	–02	–01	01	18	07	09	06	09	16	06	38	17	02
Matrix Reasoning	–02	02	06	08	–06	–01	10	05	00	02	05	18	05	–05
Picture Arrangement	00	–10	10	14	01	–09	14	06	30	–07	20	04	37	09
Symbol Search	74	72	61	78	62	62	72	65	61	63	76	19	63	70
Object Assembly	14	13	00	02	07	08	01	13	26	05	–02	10	–01	06

Note. Decimal points omitted.
[a] *Av.* = Average of 13 age groups.

or *g*. Overall, the WAIS–III is a fair measure of general intelligence, with 50 percent of its variance attributed to *g*.

The WAIS–III subtests form two clusters with respect to the measurement of *g*: (a) Vocabulary, Similarities, Information, Comprehension, Arithmetic, Block Design, and Matrix Reasoning are good measures of *g,* and (b) Symbol Search, Picture Arrangement, Letter–Number Sequencing, Picture Completion, Object Assembly, Digit Symbol—Coding, and Digit Span are fair measures of *g* (see Table N-12). The subtests in the Verbal Scale have higher *g* loadings than those in the Performance Scale (55 percent, on the average, for the Verbal subtests; 44 percent, on the average, for the Performance subtests). Highest loadings are for Vocabulary, Similarities, and Information in the Verbal Scale and for Block Design, Matrix Reasoning, and Symbol Search in the Performance Scale.

Subtest Specificity

Subtest specificity refers to the proportion of a subtest's variance that is both reliable (that is, not due to errors of measurement) and distinctive to the subtest. Although individual subtests on the WAIS–III overlap in their measurement properties (that is, the majority of the reliable variance for most subtests is common factor variance), many possess sufficient specificity at some ages to justify the interpretation of specific subtest functions (see Table N-13).

Throughout the age range covered by the WAIS–III, Arithmetic, Digit Span, Information, Digit Symbol—Coding, Block Design, and Matrix Reasoning have ample or adequate specificity. In addition, the Picture Completion subtest has ample specificity at 12 of the 13 age groups. Each of the seven remaining subtests shows a unique pattern of specificity—that is, the ages at which each has ample, adequate, or inadequate specificity differ. Vocabulary, Similarities, Comprehension, Letter–Number Sequencing, Picture Arrangement, Symbol Search, and Object Assembly have inadequate specificity at some ages.

Subtests with inadequate specificity should *not* be interpreted as measuring specific functions. These subtests, however, can be interpreted as (a) good or fair measures of *g* (see Table N-12) and (b) representing a specific factor (that is, Verbal Comprehension, Perceptual Organization, Working Memory, or Processing Speed; see Table N-11), where appropriate. The application of profile analysis also may help with the interpretation of individual subtests. (See Chapter 8 for a discussion

Table N-11
Summary of Principal Factor Analysis on WAIS–III by Age Group and for the Average of the Total Sample

Age group	Number of factors	Subtests with loadings of .30 or higher on Verbal Comprehension	Subtests with loadings of .30 or higher on Perceptual Organization	Subtests with loadings of .30 or higher on Working Memory	Subtests with loadings of .30 or higher on Processing Speed
16–17	4	V, S, A, I, C, PA	PC, BD, MR, PA, OA	A, DS, LN	CD, SS
18–19	4	V, S, A, I, C, PA	BD, OA	DS, LN, MR, PA	CD, SS
20–24	4	V, S, I, C	PC, BD, MR, PA, SS, OA	A, DS, LN	CD, SS
25–29	3	V, S, A, I, C, PA	LN, PC, BD, MR, PA, OA	DS	CD, SS
30–34	4	V, S, A, I, C, PA	PC, BD, PA, OA	A, DS, LN, MR	CD, SS
35–44	4	V, S, I, C, PA	PC, BD, MR, OA	A, DS, LN	CD, SS
45–54	4	V, S, A, C, MR	PC, BD, MR, PA, OA	DS, LN	CD, SS
55–64	4	V, S, I, C, PA	PC, BD, MR, PA, OA	A, DS, LN	CD, SS
65–69	4	V, S, A, I, C, PC	PC, BD, MR, PA, OA	A, DS, LN, MR	LN, CD, SS
70–74	4	V, S, I, C	PC, BD, MR, PA, OA	A, DS, LN, MR	PC, CD, SS
75–79	3	V, S, A, I, C	PC, BD, MR, PA, OA	A	DS, LN, CD, SS
80–84	3	V, S, A, I, C, MR, PA	PC, BD, OA	DS, LN	BD
85–89	4	V, S, I, C, PC, PA	BD, MR, OA	A, DS, LN, OA	PC, CD, SS
Av.	4	V, S, I, C, PA	PC, BD, MR, PA, OA	A, DS, LN, MR	CD, SS

Note. Abbreviations: V = Vocabulary, S = Similarities, A = Arithmetic, C = Comprehension, DS = Digit Span, I = Information, LN = Letter–Number Sequencing, PC = Picture Completion, CD = Digit Symbol—Coding, BD = Block Design, MR = Matrix Reasoning, PA = Picture Arrangement, SS = Symbol Search, Av. = Average.

of profile analysis.) Once you have determined which subtest scaled scores are significantly different from the mean of their scale and, in some cases, from one another, you may be able to draw meaningful conclusions about an examinee's cognitive strengths or weaknesses. Thus, low scores on Digit Symbol—Coding and Symbol Search and average or high scores on the other subtests may indicate difficulty in processing information rapidly. However, a high score on Digit Symbol—Coding and a low score on Symbol Search do not suggest general difficulty in processing information rapidly, because the picture is mixed.

Index Scores

The *WAIS–III Administration and Scoring Manual* and the *WAIS–III—WMS–III Technical Manual* indicate that the following combinations of subtests are the most robust for the determination of Index scores (*Index scores* is another term for *factor scores*):

Verbal Comprehension: Sum of scaled scores on Vocabulary, Similarities, and Information

Perceptual Organization: Sum of scaled scores on Picture Completion, Block Design, and Matrix Reasoning

Table N-12
WAIS–III Subtests as Measures of *g*

Subtest	Good measure of g		Subtest	Fair measure of g	
	Average loading of g	Proportion of variance attributed to g (%)		Average loading of g	Proportion of variance attributed to g (%)
Vocabulary	.83	69	Symbol Search	.70	49
Similarities	.79	62	Picture Arrangement	.66	44
Information	.79	62	Letter–Number Seq.	.65	42
Comprehension	.77	59	Picture Completion	.64	41
Arithmetic	.75	56	Object Assembly	.62	38
Block Design	.72	52	Digit Symbol—Coding	.59	35
Matrix Reasoning	.72	52	Digit Span	.57	32

Table N-13
Amount of Specificity in WAIS–III Subtests for 13 Age Groups and the Average of All Age Groups

Subtest	Age groups with ample specificity	Age groups with adequate specificity	Age groups with inadequate specificity
Vocabulary	85–89	16–17, 18–19, 20–24, 30–34, 35–44, 45–54, 55–64, 70–74, 75–79, 80–84, AV	25–29, 65–69
Similarities	16–17, 85–89	18–19, 25–29, 35–44, 45–54, 55–64, 80–84, AV	20–24, 30–34, 65–69, 70–74, 75–79
Arithmetic	16–17, 35–44, 45–54, 55–64, 70–74, 75–79, 80–84, 85–89, AVª	18–19, 20–24, 25–29, 30–34, 65–69	—
Digit Span	16–17, 18–19, 20–24, 25–29, 30–34, 35–44, 45–54, 55–64, 65–69, 70–74, 75–79, 80–84, 85–89, AV	—	—
Information	16–17	18–19, 20–24, 25–29, 30–34, 35–44, 45–54, 55–64, 65–69, 70–74, 75–79, 80–84, 85–89, AV	—
Comprehension	16–17	18–19, 20–24, 30–34, 70–74, 80–84, AV	25–29, 35–44, 45–54, 55–64, 65–69, 75–79, 85–89
Letter–Number Sequencing	30–34, 45–54, 70–74, 85–89, AV	18–19	16–17, 20–24, 25–29, 35–44, 55–64, 65–69, 75–79, 80–84
Picture Completion	16–17, 18–19, 20–24, 25–29, 30–34, 35–44, 45–54, 55–64, 65–69, 70–74, 75–79, 85–89, AV	—	80–84
Digit Symbol—Coding	16–17, 18–19, 20–24, 25–29, 30–34, 35–44, 45–54, 55–64, 65–69, 70–74, 75–79, 80–84, 85–89, AV	—	—
Block Design	16–17, 20–24, 25–29, 30–34, 35–44, 55–64, 75–79, 80–84, 85–89, AV	18–19, 45–54, 65–69, 70–74	—
Matrix Reasoning	16–17, 18–19, 20–24, 25–29, 30–34, 35–44, 45–54, 55–64, 65–69, 70–74, 75–79, 80–84, 85–89, AV	—	—
Picture Arrangement	16–17, 25–29, 35–44, 65–69, 85–89	70–74	18–19, 20–24, 30–34, 45–54, 55–64, 75–79, 80–84, AV
Symbol Search	30–34, 35–44	45–54, AV	16–17, 18–19, 20–24, 25–29, 55–64, 65–69, 70–74, 75–79, 80–84, 85–89
Object Assembly	—	45–54	16–17, 18–19, 20–24, 25–29, 30–34, 35–44, 55–64, 65–69, 70–74, 75–79, 80–84, 85–89

ª AV = Average.

Working Memory: Sum of scaled scores on Arithmetic, Digit Span, and Letter–Number Sequencing

Processing Speed: Sum of scaled scores on Digit Symbol—Coding and Symbol Search

These sums can be converted to Index scores with a mean of 100 and standard deviation of 15 (consult Tables A.6, A.7, A.8, and A.9, pp. 199–202, *WAIS–III Administration and Scoring Manual*). If there are large discrepancies among the subtests within a factor, the Index score may not provide useful information on that factor. In such cases, be extremely cautious in using the Index score. The decision to interpret an individual's WAIS–III subtest scores according to this four-factor model should be based in part on the individual's specific subtest profile. For example, it would be misleading to compute a Processing Speed Index score for scaled scores of 5 and 13 on Symbol Search and Digit Symbol—Coding, respectively, as the two scores are too dissimilar. The average score would tell us little about this factor. The specific referral questions, time constraints, and the reason for testing should help you decide whether to administer (a) the standard 11 subtests or (b) the standard 11 subtests plus the two supplementary subtests to obtain IQs and also Index scores.

In analyzing a WAIS–III protocol, use all available information about the examinee—including the referral question, her or his medical history, your observations of her or him during the examination, and other test data. Of course, you will need to understand how to interpret the test. Use the Index scores only for evaluating the examinee's strengths and weaknesses and for generating hypotheses about the examinee's abilities. When you refer to Index scores in a report, use percentile ranks to describe the examinee's performance. However, in some settings and in certain cases, you may want to report the Deviation IQs associated with the Index scores.

Ideally you should use the Index scores only at ages where the subtests have ample loadings (.30 or above) on the factor; be cautious in using the Index scores at other ages. The following list shows the ages at which it is appropriate to interpret Index scores.

• Verbal Comprehension Index score: All ages

• Perceptual Organization Index score: Ages 16–17, 20–29, 35–79 years

• Working Memory Index score: Ages 16–17, 20–24, 30–44, 55–74, 85–89 years

• Processing Speed Index score: Ages 16–79, 85–89 years

RANGE OF SUBTEST SCORES

The WAIS–III provides a range of scaled scores from 1 to 19. The test is constructed so that, even if examinees fail every item on every subtest, they are awarded at least 1 scaled-score point. On two subtests (Picture Arrangement and Object Assembly), examinees are awarded 2 or more scaled-score points, depending on their age, even if they fail all items. For example, on Picture Arrangement, examinees are awarded 2 points at ages 55–64 years, 3 points at ages 65–74 years, 4 points at ages 75–84 years, and 5 points at ages 85–89 years. On Object Assembly, examinees are given 2 scaled-score points when they fail all items if they are between 70 and 89 years of age. Thus, the range of subtest scores from 1 to 19 does not apply to all subtests at all ages.

Table N-14 shows the maximum possible scaled score for each subtest by age group. The fact that the test does not have the same maximum scaled score throughout affects primarily interpretation of the profiles of gifted examinees. You can apply profile analysis techniques appropriately at all ages for seven subtests only—Digit Span, Comprehension, Letter–Number Sequencing, Digit Symbol—Coding, Block Design, Symbol Search, and Object Assembly. *Applying profile analysis uniformly to all subtests would be misleading in some individual cases because the examinee cannot obtain the same number of scaled-score points on all subtests.* However, the failure to have the same scaled-score range at all age groups and for all subtests is usually only a minor difficulty because most subtests have a scaled-score range of at least 1 to 17.

RANGE OF FULL SCALE IQs

The range of WAIS–III Full Scale IQs for all age groups is 45 to 155. This range is insufficient for moderately to severely retarded examinees and for extremely gifted individuals. The

Table N-14
Maximum WAIS–III Subtest Scaled Scores by Age Group

Subtest	Maximum scaled score	Age group
Vocabulary	19	16–34, 70–89
	18	35–69
Similarities	19	16–24, 65–89
	18	25–34, 55–64
	17	35–54
Arithmetic	19	16–17, 70–89
	18	18–24, 55–69
	17	25–54
Digit Span	19	16–89
Information	19	16–24, 70–89
	18	25–69
Comprehension	19	16–89
Letter–Number Seq.	19	16–89
Picture Completion	19	75–89
	18	16–74
Digit Symbol—Coding	19	16–89
Block Design	19	16–89
Matrix Reasoning	19	45–89
	18	20–44
	17	16–19
Picture Arrangement	19	16–19, 55–89
	18	35–54
	17	20–34
Symbol Search	19	16–89
Object Assembly	19	16–89

WAIS–III is designed so that every examinee receives at least 11 scaled-score points for giving *no* correct answers to any subtest. Because this is potentially problematic, the *WAIS–III Administration and Scoring Manual* recommends that you compute an IQ on the Verbal Scale only when the examinee obtains raw scores greater than 0 on at least three Verbal subtests. Likewise, that manual indicates that you should compute a Performance IQ only when the examinee earns raw scores greater than 0 on at least three Performance subtests. Finally, the manual says that you should compute a Full Scale IQ only when the examinee obtains raw scores greater than 0 on three Verbal *and* three Performance subtests. This is a rule of thumb, not an empirically based recommendation, but it is useful. However, validity data are needed to show whether or not this procedure or other procedures are valid for computing IQs. The two WAIS–III manuals provide no validity data to support this recommendation.

If we follow the above recommendation, what is the lowest possible IQ that an individual can receive? If an examinee who is 27 years old obtains raw scores of 1 on the Similarities, Digit Span, Comprehension, Picture Completion, Matrix Reasoning, and Block Design subtests and raw scores of 0 on the remaining five subtests, the resulting IQs will be as follows: Verbal Scale IQ = 48 (6 scaled-score points), Performance Scale IQ = 47 (5 scaled-score points), and Full Scale IQ = 45 (11 scaled-score points). Six 1-point successes thus yield an IQ of 45.

In the case of an examinee who is 80 years old or older, the lowest Full Scale IQ that can be obtained is 48, not 45, when the examinee obtains the following scores: raw scores of 1 on the Similarities, Digit Span, Comprehension, Picture Completion, Matrix Reasoning, and Picture Arrangement subtests and raw scores of 0 on the remaining five subtests. The resulting IQs will be as follows: Verbal Scale IQ = 51 (9 scaled-score points), Performance Scale IQ = 54 (12 scaled-score points), and Full Scale IQ = 48 (21 scaled-score points). Six 1-point successes thus yield an IQ of 48.

Both of the preceding examples indicate that the WAIS–III may not provide precise IQs for individuals who are functioning at two or more standard deviations below the mean of the scale, because the scale does not sample a sufficient range of cognitive abilities for very low-functioning individuals. If an examinee fails most of the items on the WAIS–III, consider administering another intelligence test that may give you a more accurate estimate of his or her level of cognitive ability.

COMPARISON OF THE WAIS–III AND WAIS–R

Although similar to its predecessor, the WAIS–III differs from the WAIS–R in some important ways.

1. As previously noted, the revision contains three new subtests. Matrix Reasoning replaces Object Assembly as a standard subtest of the Performance Scale; the latter is

now an optional subtest. Letter–Number Sequencing and Symbol Search are new supplementary subtests.

2. The Digit Symbol—Coding subtest includes two new supplementary procedures: Digit Symbol—Incidental Learning and Digit Symbol—Copy. On the WAIS–R, this subtest involved only copying of symbols; there was no recall procedure.

3. Full-color illustrations are used in the WAIS–III.

4. The age range of the WAIS–III now extends to 89 years; in the WAIS–R, the oldest age was 74 years.

5. The WAIS–III contains four factors—Verbal Comprehension, Perceptual Organization, Working Memory, and Processing Speed—whereas the WAIS–R contained only the first two of these factors plus an additional factor called Freedom from Distractibility.

6. Scoring guidelines and administrative procedures for most subtests have been modified in the revision. For example, changes have been made in the order in which subtests are administered, order of items, starting points, discontinuance criteria, and allotment of bonus points.

7. When examinees earn raw scores of 0 on all 11 subtests, the Full Scale IQ score extends to 45 at all 13 age groups in the standardization sample. In the WAIS–R, a Full Scale IQ of 45 could be obtained only at ages 18–19 years, 20–24 years, and 25–34 years.

8. The revision deemphasizes speed of performance within the Performance Scale and the Full Scale, but then places more emphasis on speed of performance by having a separate measure of processing speed.

9. The revision places increased emphasis on measuring fluid intelligence and working memory.

10. The number of items has been increased on Picture Completion, Digit Symbol—Coding, Similarities, Block Design, Arithmetic, Digit Span, Picture Arrangement, Comprehension, and Object Assembly and decreased on Vocabulary and Information.

Table N-15 highlights the changes in the WAIS–III.

ADMINISTERING THE WAIS–III

The procedures discussed in Chapter 5 for administering psychological tests will help you administer the WAIS–III, as will the guidelines in Appendix I (pages 1051–1074) for administering the WISC–III. However, you must master the special procedures developed for the WAIS–III, whether or not you are familiar with the WISC–III. Be careful not to confuse the administration procedures for the WISC–III or the WAIS–R with those for the WAIS–III —some subtests with the same name have different standardized instructions and time limits. The general problems in administering the WISC–III also apply to the WAIS–III. Here are some potential problems.

1. Reading questions too quickly or too slowly.
2. Not enunciating clearly.
3. Leaving unessential materials on the table.
4. Failing to adequately shield the test protocol or the contents of the test manual from the examinee's view.
5. Not recording all responses.
6. Calculating chronological age incorrectly.
7. Not adhering to guidelines for giving help.
8. Not adhering to standardized instructions.
9. Ignoring proper time limits.
10. Not questioning ambiguous or vague responses.
11. Not crediting responses.
12. Not following starting rules.
13. Not following discontinuance rules.
14. Making errors in converting raw scores to scaled scores.
15. Prorating incorrectly.
16. Giving time-bonus credits incorrectly.
17. Using inappropriate norms.
18. Failing to give a score of 0 to an incorrect response.
19. Adding raw scores incorrectly.
20. Adding scaled scores inaccurately.
21. Not checking all Digit Symbol—Coding responses.
22. Failing to credit items not administered below the starting point.

Table N-15
Highlights of Changes in WAIS–III

Area or subtest	Changes from WAIS–R	Area or subtest	Changes from WAIS–R
Age range	Extended 15 years to cover the age range from 16-0 to 89-11.	Record Form (*Continued*)	contains Symbol Search, Digit Symbol—Incidental Learning, and Digit Symbol—Copy. On Digit Symbol—Coding, the space between the key and stimulus items was increased to reduce the possibility that left-handed individuals will cover the key as they work. Increased space is provided to record behavioral observations. Unlike the WAIS–R, the WAIS–III does not ask for examinee's occupation, ethnicity, handedness, or place of examination.
Standardization	1995 census data used, and the sample was increased from 1,880 to 2,450 participants.		
Stratification variables	Generally similar, but the number of age groups was increased from 9 to 13 and residence and occupational variables were dropped.	Types of scores	Provides IQs ($M = 100$, $SD = 15$) for Verbal, Performance, and Full Scales; Index scores ($M = 100$, $SD = 15$) for four factors; percentile ranks for IQs and Index scores; subtest scaled scores; discrepancy scores for IQs and Index scores; and deviation scores for the 14 subtests. WAIS–R provided IQs for Verbal, Performance, and Full Scales, along with scaled scores and age-corrected scores for the 11 subtests.
Number of subtests	14 instead of 11, with Matrix Reasoning, Number–Letter Sequencing, and Symbol Search added.		
Optional procedures	Two new optional procedures added: Digit Symbol—Incidental Learning and Digit Symbol—Copy.		
Reliability	Reliability coefficients generally higher than those for the WAIS–R.		
Validity	Validity coefficients generally similar to those for the WAIS–R.	Confidence intervals	Confidence intervals in the *WAIS–III Administration and Scoring Manual* are based on the estimated true score method; no confidence intervals are given in the WAIS–R manual.
Scoring examples	Somewhat expanded and placed with the subtest proper instead of in the back of the manual.		
General administrative changes	Order of administering subtests changed, item order changed on some subtests, starting points changed on some subtests, samples added on some subtests, discontinuance criteria changed on some subtests, bonus-point allotment changed on some subtests, and easier items added to most subtests.	Factor structure	The manual proposes a model with four factors (Verbal Comprehension, Perceptual Organization, Working Memory, and Processing Speed) that differ from the three factors found on the WAIS–R.
		g loading	About the same as on the WAIS–R.
		Art work	Color is used instead of black and white for Picture Completion and Matrix Reasoning subtests; some visual stimuli have been enlarged; art work has a more contemporary appearance.
Computation of IQ	No change, but WAIS–III manual stipulates that three Verbal and three Performance subtests must have raw scores greater than 0.		
		Test-retest changes	Retest changes are generally comparable on the WAIS–III and WAIS–R.
Intelligence classification and range	Uses "Extremely Low" instead of "Mentally Retarded" to classify IQs below 70.	Ceiling to floor level of IQ	The range of IQs is 45 to 155 on the WAIS–III for all age groups; on the WAIS–R, it was from 45 to 150, but not for all age groups.
Record Form	Last four pages of the Record Form are a profile page, score conversion page, discrepancy analysis page, and demographics page. Allows for the determination of subtest strengths and weaknesses and confidence limits. More space is provided to write responses for Information, Comprehension, Vocabulary, and Similarities. Starting points, discontinuance rules, time limits, and prompts to help facilitate administration are included. A separate booklet	Subtests for which scaled scores of 1 to 19 are available	More subtests have a range of 1 to 19 scaled-score points on the WAIS–III than on the WAIS–R.
		Picture Completion	Contains 25 instead of 20 items, with 10 modified and 15 new items. All pictures are

(Continued)

Table N-15 (*Continued*)

Area or subtest	Changes from WAIS–R	Area or subtest	Changes from WAIS–R
Picture Completion (*Continued*)	enlarged and in color. Five reversal items lower the floor of the subtest. Querying guidelines have been clarified and expanded.	Digit Span	Contains 15 instead of 14 sets of digits, with one 2-digit set added to Digits Forward. Supplementary norms are provided for Digits Forward, Digits Backward, and Digits Forward minus Backward for each age group in the standardization sample.
Vocabulary	Contains 33 instead of 35 items, with 25 retained and 8 new items. Administration has been changed so that words are presented orally and also displayed in a stimulus book. A reverse sequence procedure is used if an examinee does not obtain perfect scores on the first two items given. The discontinuance rule has been changed from five to six consecutive failures. Additional scoring examples are provided.	Information	Contains 28 instead of 29 items, with 19 retained and 9 new items (2 easy, 7 hard). A procedure for administering items in reverse sequence has been added for examinees who miss item 5 or 6. The discontinuance rule has been changed from five to six consecutive scores of 0. Additional sample scoring items have been included.
Digit Symbol— Coding	Contains one additional row. Symbols have been slightly enlarged, and the name of the subtest has changed. The time limit has been changed from 90 seconds to 120 seconds.	Picture Arrangement	Contains 11 instead of 10 items, with 5 modified and 6 new items (2 easy, 4 hard). Five items have 1-point scores for plausible alternative arrangements; the WAIS–R had four such items. Stimuli have been enlarged and printed on card stock.
Similarities	Contains 19 instead of 14 items, with 11 retained and 8 new items. The first five items (reversal items) are given only to examinees who fail to obtain perfect scores on items 6 and 7. Additional sample scoring items are provided.	Comprehension	Contains 18 instead of 16 items, with 12 retained and 6 new items (2 easy, 4 hard). The subtest begins with item 4; if the examinee does not obtain perfect scores on items 4 and 5, items 1–3 are given in reverse order to meet the basal requirement. More sample scoring items are provided.
Block Design	Contains 14 instead of 9 items, with 9 retained and 5 new items (4 easy, 1 difficult). Easy items are administered in reverse order to obtain a basal if an examinee fails or obtains only 1 point on items 5 and 6. Changes have been made in bonus-point allotment; designs have been enlarged.	Symbol Search	New supplementary subtest containing 60 items. It may be substituted for Digit Symbol—Coding in IQ computation if that subtest has been spoiled.
Arithmetic	Contains 20 instead of 14 items, with all WAIS–R items retained (some with wording changes) and 6 items added. Four easy items are administered in reverse order to examinees who obtain a score of 0 on item 5 or 6. Bonus points are given for speed on items 19 and 20 only.	Letter–Number Sequencing	New supplementary subtest containing 7 sets of number-letter combinations. It may be substituted for Digit Span in IQ computation if that subtest has been spoiled.
Matrix Reasoning	New 26-item untimed subtest replaces Object Assembly for computation of the Performance IQ. Each item consists of a matrix from which a section is missing and five response choices.	Object Assembly	Optional subtest may be substituted for any Performance subtest for individuals 16–74 years old. Contains 5 instead of 4 items, with 3 retained and 2 new items. The layout shield is now freestanding.

23. Giving credit for items missed above the starting point.
24. Not scoring a subtest.
25. Converting scaled scores to IQs incorrectly.

26. Including a supplementary subtest, in addition to the six standard subtests in the Verbal Scale and five standard subtests in the Performance Scale, to compute an IQ.

27. Using both Digit Symbol—Coding and Symbol Search to compute an IQ.
28. Substituting Letter–Number Sequencing for a subtest other than Digit Span to compute an IQ.
29. Substituting Symbol Search for a subtest other than Digit Symbol—Coding to compute an IQ.

Study the instructions in the *WAIS–III Administration and Scoring Manual* and become thoroughly familiar with the test materials before you give the test. Although the Verbal subtests are generally easier to administer than the Performance subtests, they are more difficult to score. You should use a stopwatch when you administer the timed WAIS–III subtests. Also, assign tentative scores as you administer the test, and then rescore each item after you finish administering the test. If you are unsure how to score a response during the test proper and the item is needed to establish a starting point (also referred to as a basal level) or discontinuance point (also referred to as a ceiling level), always err on the side of administering other items, even though these items may not be critical to establishing the starting or discontinuance point. You don't want to invalidate the test by failing to establish a basal level or ceiling level.

The Record Form should be clearly and accurately completed— *record all responses relevant to the test and testing situation verbatim.* You need to check all calculations carefully, including the conversion of raw scores to scaled scores and scaled scores to IQs and Index scores. In converting raw scores to scaled scores, be aware that the order of subtests on the Score Conversion Page (p. 12 of the Record Form) is not the same as the order of subtests in Table A.1 (pp. 181–194) in the *WAIS–III Administration and Scoring Manual*. On the Score Conversion Page the subtests appear in the order in which they are administered, whereas in Table A.1 the subtests are ordered by scale—the seven Verbal subtests in the upper half of the table and the seven Performance subtests in the lower half. Be sure to use the appropriate column in Table A.1 for converting raw scores to scaled scores. For example, to convert a raw score on Picture Completion (the first subtest administered) to a scaled score, you must use the column in the lower half of Table A.1 (Performance Subtests) that shows raw scores for the Picture Completion subtest and its corresponding scaled scores. The suggestions in Ex-

hibit N-1 and the checklist in Exhibit N-2 also should help you learn how to administer the WAIS–III.

Physical Abilities Required for the WAIS–III

Examinees need to have adequate hearing and language functioning in order to be administered the Verbal Scale subtests, and adequate vision and visual-motor ability in order to be administered the Performance Scale subtests. The suggestions presented in Appendix I (pages 1072–1074) for administering the WISC–III to disabled examinees should be studied carefully.

Auditory functions. Examinees with an undiagnosed hearing deficit may obtain low scores because they fail to understand the instructions and questions, not because of cognitive limitations. Sometimes examinees may have a temporary hearing loss due to allergies, sinus infections, colds, or other intermittent ear, nose, and throat problems. You will need to consider the following questions in evaluating the examinee's auditory ability: How well does the examinee understand conversation when the speaker is outside of the examinee's field of vision? Does the examinee watch the speaker's mouth intently during conversation? Is there evidence that the examinee has an auditory discrimination deficit (e.g., mistakes *winter* for *winner*)? Does the examinee frequently need to have instructions repeated? When the volume of speech is increased, does the examinee's comprehension of spoken language improve? In cases where a significant hearing problem is documented or suspected, ask the examinee to repeat a few complex sentences before you administer the test (e.g., "The lawyer's closing argument convinced him"). If the examinee repeats the sentences correctly, you can be reasonably confident that his or her hearing proficiency is sufficient for you to administer the WAIS–III. Conversely, if the examinee fails to repeat the sentences correctly, you might want to recommend that he or she receive a hearing evaluation and postpone administering the test until you obtain the evaluation results. If the examinee usually wears a hearing aid, be sure that he or she wears it during the examination and verifies for you that it is in good operating order.

Exhibit N-1
Supplementary Instructions for Administering the WAIS–III

1. Study and practice administering the test repeatedly before you give it to an examinee to fulfill a class assignment.

2. Organize your test materials before the examinee comes into the room. Make sure that all test materals—including stimulus booklets, blocks, cards, puzzle pieces, Record Form, Response Booklet, stopwatch, and pencils—are in the kit. Arrange the Picture Arrangement cards in numerical sequence. Have extra blank paper to make notes if needed.

3. Complete the top of page 1 of the Record Form (examinee's name, examiner's name, examinee's age, and date of testing) and the top of page 14 (Demographics Page) of the Record Form (date tested, date of examinee's birth, age, name, ID, sex, address, highest level of education, and examiner's name). It also is a good idea to add the examinee's occupation. If you have this information available, it saves time to enter it in advance.

4. Calculate the chronological age (CA) and put it in the box provided on the Demographics Page (page 14 of the Record Form). For testing purposes, months are considered to have 30 days. Also, note that days of age are not rounded up to the nearest month. Thus, the age 19 years 11 months 29 days is 19 years 11 months, not 20 years 0 months.

5. Before beginning the first subtest, introduce the scale using the explanation on page 63 of the *WAIS–III Administration and Scoring Manual*. Use your judgment in deciding whether the examinee needs further explanation of the reason for the examination. However, try not to use the word *intelligence,* because telling the examinee that he or she is about to take an intelligence test may cause unnecessary anxiety and negatively affect his or her performance.

6. Administer the subtests in the order presented in the *WAIS–III Administration and Scoring Manual*, except in rare circumstances. Do not change the wording of the directions or the wording of questions on any subtest. Read the directions and items verbatim from the *WAIS–III Administration and Scoring Manual*. This means that you do *not* omit words, introduce new words, or ad lib.

7. Start with the appropriate item in each subtest, and follow all basal and discontinuance criteria. You must be knowledgeable about the scoring criteria before you administer the test.

8. Record verbatim all of the examinee's responses that are pertinent to the test, testing situation, or referral question or that are otherwise helpful in understanding the examinee. Write clearly and do not use unusual abbreviations. Record the time accurately in the spaces provided in the Record Form.

9. Question all ambiguous, incomplete, or unscorable responses, using the directions or instructions suggested in the *WAIS–III Administration and Scoring Manual* for questioning. Write a (Q) after each questioned response. Question all responses followed by a (Q) in the *WAIS–III Administration and Scoring Manual*.

10. If an examinee says "I don't know" to an item but then passes more difficult items on the same subtest, readminister the earlier item after the examinee has reached the ceiling level if you believe that he or she may know the answer to that item.

11. If an examinee says "I can't do it" or stops working on an item before the time limit has expired, gently urge her or him to proceed by saying "Just try once more, see if you can do it" or "Try it just a little longer."

12. Carefully score each protocol, recheck scoring, and transfer subtest scores to the Score Conversion Page (p. 12 of the Record Form) under the column labeled Raw Score.

13. If a subtest was spoiled, write *spoiled* by the subtest total score and on the Score Conversion Page where you entered the raw scores and scaled scores. If you did not administer a subtest, write *NA* in the margin of the Record Form and on the Score Conversion Page.

14. Transform raw scores into scaled scores through use of Table A.1 (pp. 181–194) in the *WAIS–III Administration and Scoring Manual*. Be sure to use the page of Table A.1 that is appropriate for the examinee's age and the correct row and column for each transformation. If you also use the scaled scores based on the reference group of persons aged 20–34 years old (p. 194 of the manual), be sure they are entered in the appropriate column on the Score Conversion Page. *Never use the reference group scaled scores to compute IQs or Index scores.*

15. Add the scaled scores for the six standard Verbal subtests to compute the sum of the scaled scores. Do not use Letter–Number Sequencing to compute the Verbal score unless you have substituted it for Digit Span. Add the scaled scores for the five standard Performance subtests. Do not include Symbol Search or Object Assembly unless you have substituted Symbol Search for Digit Symbol—Coding or Object Assembly for another Performance subtest. Sum the Verbal and the Performance subtest scaled scores to obtain the sum for the Full Scale. Recheck your addition on all subtests and scales.

16. Administer the Letter–Number Sequencing and Symbol Search subtests if you want to obtain Index scores. Do not use these two subtests to compute IQs when you administer the six standard Verbal Scale and five standard Performance Scale subtests.

17. Substitute the Letter–Number Sequencing subtest to compute the Verbal and Full Scale IQs if the Digit Span subtest is spoiled or if you did not administer it. Similarly, substitute Symbol Search to compute the Performance and Full Scale IQ if the Digit Symbol—Coding subtest is spoiled or if you did not administer it. Substitute the Object Assembly subtest to compute the Performance and Full Scale IQ if any of the standard Performance Scale subtests were not administered.

18. Obtain the IQs from Tables A.3 through A.5 (pp. 195–198) of the WAIS–III Administration and Scoring Manual. There are tables for the Verbal Scale (A.3), the Performance Scale (A.4), and the Full Scale (A.5). Obtain the Index scores from Tables A.6 through A.9. Be sure to use

(Continued)

Exhibit N-1 (*Continued*)

the correct table for each of the three IQs and each of the four Index scores. Record the IQs and Index scores on the Profile Page of the Record Form (p. 11). Next, re-check all of your work. If any IQs were obtained by use of a short form, write *SF* beside the appropriate IQs. If any IQs were prorated, write *PRO* beside the appropriate IQs. If fewer than five subtests were administered in the Verbal Scale or fewer than four subtests were administered in the Performance Scale, use the Tellegen and Briggs short form procedure, described on page 138 of the text, to compute the IQ. You also can consult Tables O-7 through O-11 in this text. These tables provide estimated Full Scale Deviation Quotients for several short forms based on the Tellegen and Briggs procedure.

19. If you would like, plot the IQ scores, Index scores, and subtest scores on the graph provided on the Profile Page of the Record Form.

20. Obtain a percentile for each IQ and Index score from Tables A.3 through A.9 in the *WAIS–III Administration and Scoring Manual*.

21. Obtain a confidence interval for each IQ and Index score from Table O-1 of this text.

22. Complete the appropriate part of the Score Conversion Page (p. 12) of the Record Form to determine the examinee's strengths and weaknesses for the individual subtests. Enter the scaled scores in the appropriate spaces

for the subtests you administered, and follow the instructions given on pages 60 and 61 in the *WAIS–III Administration and Scoring Manual*.

23. Complete the Discrepancy Analysis Page (p. 13) of the Record Form to compute the discrepancy between the Verbal and Performance IQs and the differences between all combinations of the Index scores. Evaluate the statistical significance of each difference, and note the frequency with which each difference was found in the standardization sample. Also note the difference between the longest Digits Forward and the longest Digits Backward on Digit Span. Follow the instructions for analyzing score discrepancies provided on pages 61 to 62 in the *WAIS–III Administration and Scoring Manual*. *We suggest, however, that you divide all of the frequencies in Table B.2 by 2 when you complete the last column of the Discrepancy Analysis Page, which is called "Frequency of difference in standardization sample," to get the appropriate estimated base rate.*

24. In summary, read the directions verbatim, enunciate clearly and pronounce words correctly, query at the appropriate times, start with the appropriate item, obtain a basal where needed, discontinue at the appropriate location, use correct timing, arrange items properly before the examinee, and follow the specific administration guidelines in the *WAIS–III Administration and Scoring Manual*.

Language functions. Note any language difficulties that the examinee may have. Always consider the examinee's age and ethnicity and what is normal language for her or his age group. For adolescents and adults, normal speech is fluent (i.e., produced with little or no effort, about 100 to 125 words per minute, with phrases of 5 or more words strung together between pauses; Albert, Goodglass, Helm, Rubens, & Alexander, 1981) and is free of articulation difficulties, gross grammatical errors, and word substitutions. In contrast, abnormal speech may be nonfluent (i.e., slow, laboriously produced, with shortened phrase length) and contain incorrect word substitutions (e.g., the examinee says *writer* instead of *pencil*) and grammatical errors. Here are some informal procedures that are helpful in gauging the examinee's language ability:

• Ask the examinee to perform several simple actions (e.g., "Place the book on the table").

• Ask the examinee to answer simple factual questions (e.g., "Is a hammer good for painting the house?").

• Ask the examinee to name simple objects (e.g., pencil, watch, finger) that you show to him or her.

If the tasks you give to the examinee are age-appropriate, difficulty in performing any of them (including difficulty in following verbal commands, answering simple questions of fact, or naming common objects) suggests impaired language comprehension or naming difficulties. Such failures are sometimes noted in examinees who have aphasia (see Chapter 22).

It will be difficult to obtain valid scores on the Verbal Scale subtests when examinees have either significant language comprehension deficits or significant language expressive difficulties, such as dysnomia (i.e., naming difficulties) or other language production difficulties. However, language-impaired examinees should be able to take the Performance Scale subtests if they understand the instructions. You may communicate instructions nonverbally, through gesture or by performing simple actions that the examinee imitates. Appendix D (page 896) provides some guidelines. For example, to

Exhibit N-2
Administrative Checklist for the WAIS–III

ADMINISTRATIVE CHECKLIST FOR THE WAIS–III

Name of examiner: _____

Date: _____

Name of examinee: _____

Name of observer: _____

(Note: *If an item is not applicable, mark NA to the left of the number.*)

Picture Completion	*Circle One*	
1. Reads directions verbatim	Yes	No
2. Reads directions clearly	Yes	No
3. Pronounces words in queries clearly	Yes	No
4. Places booklet flat on table, close to examinee	Yes	No
5. Begins with item 6	Yes	No
6. Begins timing after last word of instructions	Yes	No
7. Allows a maximum of 20 seconds on each item	Yes	No
8. Gives the prompt "Yes, but what's missing?" only once	Yes	No
9. Gives the prompt "Something is missing in the picture. What is it that is missing?" only once	Yes	No
10. Gives the prompt "Yes, but what is the most important part that is missing?" only once	Yes	No
11. If the examinee fails item 6, responds by saying "You see the doorknob is missing"	Yes	No
12. If the examinee fails item 7, responds by saying "You see the nose piece is missing"	Yes	No
13. Administers items in reverse order when examinee scores 0 on item 6 or 7	Yes	No
14. Attempts to establish a basal level	Yes	No
15. Inquires correctly on items 8, 10, and 19	Yes	No
16. Allows credit for items not administered when those items precede two consecutive successes	Yes	No
17. Allows credit for a correct spoken or pointing response	Yes	No
18. Allows 1 point credit for each correct response	Yes	No
19. Allows no credit for correct responses given after time limit	Yes	No
20. Records 0 or 1 point for each item	Yes	No
21. Discontinues subtest after five consecutive failures	Yes	No
22. Adds points correctly	Yes	No

Comments: _____

_____

_____

Vocabulary	*Circle One*	
1. Reads directions verbatim	Yes	No
2. Reads directions clearly	Yes	No
3. Pronounces words clearly	Yes	No
4. Places booklet flat on table, close to examinee	Yes	No
5. Begins with item 4	Yes	No
6. Allows sufficient time for examinee to respond to each word	Yes	No
7. Queries every response followed in the WAIS–III manual by a (Q), even if it is a 0-point response	Yes	No
8. Queries vague responses	Yes	No
9. Does not query a clearcut response, especially one that is not followed by a (Q) in the WAIS–III manual	Yes	No
10. Administers items 1–3 in reverse order when examinee fails or gives a 1-point response to item 4 or 5	Yes	No
11. Attempts to establish a basal level	Yes	No
12. Inquires about vague responses, regionalisms, or slang responses	Yes	No
13. Limits inquiries to "Tell me more about it" or "Explain what you mean"	Yes	No
14. Allows 1 or 2 points credit for each correct response	Yes	No
15. Records 0, 1, or 2 points, as appropriate	Yes	No
16. Discontinues after six consecutive failures	Yes	No
17. Adds points correctly	Yes	No

Comments: _____

_____

_____

(*Continued*)

Exhibit N-2 (*Continued*)

Digit Symbol—Coding

		Circle One
1.	Reads directions verbatim	Yes No
2.	Reads directions clearly	Yes No
3.	Provides two No. 2 graphite pencils without erasers	Yes No
4.	Provides a smooth work surface	Yes No
5.	Points to the key while reading the first part of the instructions	Yes No
6.	Points to the proper boxes, numbers, and symbols while reading the instructions	Yes No
7.	Follows directions in manual for pointing to sample items while reading directions	Yes No
8.	Does not time sample items	Yes No
9.	Gives proper instructions after examinee completes the sample items and clearly understands the task	Yes No
10.	Praises examinee's successes on each sample item by saying "Yes" or "Right"	Yes No
11.	Corrects examinee's mistakes on sample items	Yes No
12.	Explains use of key again if examinee fails the sample items	Yes No
13.	Does not begin the subtest until the examinee clearly understands the task	Yes No
14.	Provides proper caution the first time the examinee omits an item or does only one type: first says "Do them in order. Don't skip any," and then points to the next item and says "Do this one next"	Yes No
15.	Reminds the examinee to continue until told to stop (when needed)	Yes No
16.	Begins timing immediately after completing instructions	Yes No
17.	Allows 120 seconds	Yes No
18.	Records time accurately	Yes No
19.	Uses scoring stencil to score the subtest	Yes No
20.	Does not give credit to the sample items, incorrectly drawn items, or items completed out of sequence	Yes No
21.	Records the correct number of items	Yes No
22.	If Digit Symbol—Incidental Learning is administered and examinee fails to complete four rows within 120 seconds, marks examinee's progress at 120 seconds and allows additional time for examinee to work to the end of the fourth row	Yes No
23.	Reads directions verbatim on Digit Symbol—Incidental Learning	Yes No
24.	Has examinee write answers in Response Booklet	Yes No
25.	Uses cardboard or opaque paper to cover pairing items	Yes No
26.	Presents Free Recall task by pointing to the blank area at the bottom of the page	Yes No
27.	Administers the Digit Symbol—Copy task after examinee completes the last subtest	Yes No

Comments: _____

_____

_____

Similarities

		Circle One
1.	Reads directions verbatim	Yes No
2.	Reads directions clearly	Yes No
3.	Reads items verbatim and clearly	Yes No
4.	Begins with item 6	Yes No
5.	Allows sufficient time for examinee to answer each question	Yes No
6.	Gives example of 2-point response if examinee gives 1-point response to item 6	Yes No
7.	Says "They are both musical instruments" if examinee gives a 0-point response to item 6	Yes No
8.	Administers items 1–5 in reverse order if examinee fails or obtains a score of 1 on item 6 or 7	Yes No
9.	Attempts to establish a basal level	Yes No
10.	Queries every response followed in the WAIS–III manual by a (Q), even if it is a 0-point response	Yes No
11.	Queries vague responses	Yes No
12.	Says "What do you mean?" or "Tell me more about it" if examinee's response is unclear	Yes No
13.	Does not query a clearcut response	Yes No
14.	Asks "Now which one is it?" each time an examinee's response contains both a correct and an incorrect answer	Yes No
15.	Assigns 1 point credit for each correct response to items 1–5	Yes No
16.	Assigns 1 or 2 points credit for each correct response to items 6–19	Yes No
17.	Records 0, 1, or 2 points, as appropriate	Yes No
18.	Discontinues after four consecutive failures	Yes No
19.	Assigns credit for items not administered when those items precede perfect scores on two consecutive items	Yes No
20.	Adds points correctly	Yes No

(*Continued*)

Exhibit N-2 (*Continued*)

Comments: _____

_____

_____

Block Design	*Circle One*	
1. Reads directions verbatim	Yes	No
2. Reads directions clearly	Yes	No
3. Turns blocks slowly to show different sides as instructions are read	Yes	No
4. Begins with item 5	Yes	No
5. Places blocks and cards properly	Yes	No
6. Constructs model and places Stimulus Booklet approximately 7 inches from the edge of the table closest to the examinee	Yes	No
7. Places model or Stimulus Booklet a little to the left of the examinee's midline for right-handed examinees and a little to the right of midline for left-handed examinees	Yes	No
8. Constructs items 5 and 6 properly	Yes	No
9. Administers items 1–4 in reverse order if examinee fails or obtains 1 point on item 5 or 6	Yes	No
10. Attempts to establish a basal level	Yes	No
11. Assigns credit for items not administered when those items precede perfect scores (2 points) on two consecutive items	Yes	No
12. Presents pictures in the Stimulus Book with the unbound edge toward the examinee	Yes	No
13. Arranges blocks so that only one block has a red-and-white side facing up for the four-block designs and only three blocks have a red-and-white side facing up for the nine-block designs	Yes	No
14. Scrambles blocks between designs	Yes	No
15. Begins timing after the last word of instructions	Yes	No
16. Records time in the Record Form	Yes	No
17. Uses correct time limits	Yes	No
18. Stops timing when examinee is obviously finished with item	Yes	No
19. Allows examinee to continue working on item after time limit when examinee is nearing completion of task	Yes	No
20. Gives a second trial when examinee fails first trial on items 1–6	Yes	No
21. Does not give second trial on items 7–14	Yes	No

	Circle One	
22. Uses the correct number of blocks for each item	Yes	No
23. Says "But, you see, the blocks go this way" and corrects examinee's design the first time examinee rotates a design	Yes	No
24. Gives instructions about the need to correct a rotated design only once during the test	Yes	No
25. Assigns 2 points when the examinee gets items 5 and 6 correct on the first trial	Yes	No
26. Assigns 1 point when the examinee gets items 5 and 6 correct on the second trial	Yes	No
27. Assigns correct number of points, including time-bonus credits, for items 7–14	Yes	No
28. Assigns no credit for correct responses given after time limit	Yes	No
29. Circles, on the Record Form, a Y (Yes) or N (No) for each item	Yes	No
30. Records exact amount of time taken to solve each item	Yes	No
31. Discontinues subtest after three consecutive failures	Yes	No
32. Adds points correctly	Yes	No

Comments: _____

_____

_____

Arithmetic	*Circle One*	
1. Reads directions verbatim	Yes	No
2. Reads directions clearly	Yes	No
3. Begins with item 5	Yes	No
4. Uses correct timing	Yes	No
5. Administers items 1–4 in reverse order when item 5 or 6 is failed	Yes	No
6. Attempts to establish a basal level	Yes	No
7. Forbids examinee to use pencil and paper	Yes	No
8. Allows examinee to use a finger to "write" on the table	Yes	No
9. Records the exact amount of time required to solve each item	Yes	No
10. Begins timing immediately after each problem has been read	Yes	No
11. Repeats a problem only once	Yes	No
12. Records time from the ending of the first reading of the problem to when the response is made, even when problem is read again	Yes	No

Exhibit N-2 (*Continued*)

	Circle One	
13. Assigns no credit for correct responses given after time limit	Yes	No
14. Assigns 1 point credit for each correct response on items 1–18	Yes	No
15. Assigns 2 points credit for each correct response given within 10 seconds on items 19 and 20	Yes	No
16. Assigns credit for correct numerical quantity, even when unit is not given	Yes	No
17. Gives credit when examinee spontaneously corrects an incorrect response within time limit	Yes	No
18. Records 0, 1, or 2 points, as appropriate	Yes	No
19. Discontinues after four consecutive failures	Yes	No
20. Adds points correctly	Yes	No

Comments: _____

_____

_____

Matrix Reasoning   *Circle One*

1. Reads directions verbatim	Yes	No
2. Reads directions clearly	Yes	No
3. Begins with sample items A, B, and C	Yes	No
4. Places booklet flat on the table, close to examinee	Yes	No
5. Presents pictures in the booklet with unbound edge toward the examinee	Yes	No
6. Demonstrates the correct way to solve the problem if any sample item is failed	Yes	No
7. Proceeds to item 4 regardless of examinee's performance on sample items	Yes	No
8. Assigns full credit for items 1–3 if examinee earns perfect scores (1 point) on items 4 and 5	Yes	No
9. Administers items 1–3 in reverse sequence when examinee fails item 4 or 5	Yes	No
10. Attempts to establish a basal level	Yes	No
11. Circles examinee's numerical responses on Record Form	Yes	No
12. Discontinues subtest after four consecutive scores of 0 or four scores of 0 on five consecutive items	Yes	No
13. Adds points correctly	Yes	No

Comments: _____

_____

_____

Digit Span   *Circle One*

1. Reads directions verbatim	Yes	No

	Circle One	
2. Reads directions clearly	Yes	No
3. Begins with item 1	Yes	No
4. Administers both trials of each item	Yes	No
5. Pronounces digits singly, distinctly, at the rate of one digit per second, without chunking digits	Yes	No
6. Drops voice inflection slightly on last digit	Yes	No
7. Pauses after each sequence to allow examinee to respond	Yes	No
8. Administers Digits Backward even if examinee obtains a score of 0 on Digits Forward	Yes	No
9. Gives sample item for Digits Backward	Yes	No
10. Gives examinee the correct answer to sample item if the examinee fails the item on Digits Backward	Yes	No
11. Discontinues Digits Forward after failure on both trials of any item	Yes	No
12. Discontinues Digits Backward after failure on both trials of any item	Yes	No
13. Assigns 1 point for each trial passed	Yes	No
14. Records successes and failures on Record Form	Yes	No
15. Adds points correctly	Yes	No

Comments: _____

_____

_____

Information   *Circle One*

1. Reads directions verbatim	Yes	No
2. Reads directions clearly	Yes	No
3. Reads items verbatim and clearly	Yes	No
4. Begins with item 5	Yes	No
5. Gives sufficient time for examinee to respond to each question	Yes	No
6. Administers items 1–4 in reverse sequence when examinee fails item 5 or 6	Yes	No
7. Attempts to establish a basal level	Yes	No
8. Says "Yes, but what direction is that?" if examinee points in response to item 6	Yes	No
9. Asks "What scale?" if examinee fails to indicate which temperature scale in response to item 21	Yes	No
10. Says "Explain what you mean" or "Tell me more about it" when responses are not clear	Yes	No
11. Repeats the question when examinee's response suggests that examinee misheard or misunderstood the exact meaning of the question	Yes	No

(*Continued*)

Exhibit N-2 (*Continued*)

12. Assigns credit for correct responses made after the inquiry	Yes	No
13. Avoids asking leading questions or spelling words	Yes	No
14. Assigns credit for items not administered when those items precede two consecutive successes	Yes	No
15. Assigns 1 point credit for each correct response	Yes	No
16. Records 0 or 1 point for each item	Yes	No
17. Discontinues after six consecutive failures	Yes	No
18. Adds points correctly	Yes	No

Comments: _____

_____

_____

Picture Arrangement

Circle One

1. Reads directions verbatim	Yes	No
2. Reads directions clearly	Yes	No
3. Begins with item 1 in all cases	Yes	No
4. Has cards prearranged in numerical sequence and places all cards in correct numerical order from examinee's left to examinee's right	Yes	No
5. If examinee fails trial 1 of item, proceeds to trial 2	Yes	No
6. Rearranges cards in trial 1 in correct order by moving cards one at a time to a new row and then points to each card as story is told	Yes	No
7. Rearranges cards in trial 1 in original numerical order and says "Now you put them in the right order"	Yes	No
8. Begins timing after last word of instructions	Yes	No
9. Records exact amount of time taken to complete each item or trial	Yes	No
10. Records in the Response Order column of the Record Form the exact order in which examinee arranges the cards	Yes	No
11. Stops timing when examinee is obviously finished or when time limit has expired on each item	Yes	No
12. Does not give a second trial on items 2–11	Yes	No
13. Uses correct time limits	Yes	No
14. Assigns 2 points credit for a correct response given to item 1, trial 1	Yes	No
15. Assigns 1 point credit for a correct response given to item 1, trial 2	Yes	No
16. Allows examinee to continue working on arrangement after time limit has expired when examinee is nearing completion of task	Yes	No

17. Assigns no credit for correct responses given after time limit	Yes	No
18. Gives correct number of credit points on each item	Yes	No
19. Discontinues after four consecutive failures	Yes	No
20. Adds points correctly	Yes	No

Comments: _____

_____

_____

Comprehension

Circle One

1. Reads directions verbatim	Yes	No
2. Reads directions clearly	Yes	No
3. Begins with item 4	Yes	No
4. If examinee earns full credit (2 points) on items 4 and 5, gives full credit for items 1–3	Yes	No
5. If examinee obtains a score of 0 or 1 on item 4 or 5, administers items 1–3 in reverse sequence	Yes	No
6. Attempts to establish a basal level	Yes	No
7. Repeats question if examinee requests or has not responded after 10–15 seconds	Yes	No
8. Encourages hesitant examinee to speak by saying "Yes" or "Go ahead"	Yes	No
9. Queries every response followed in the WAIS–III manual by a (Q), even if it is a 0-point response	Yes	No
10. Queries vague or ambiguous responses, saying "Explain what you mean" or "Tell me more about it"	Yes	No
11. Does not query a clearcut response	Yes	No
12. Prompts for second response on items 5, 6, 7, 10, and 13 only when first response is correct	Yes	No
13. Prompts for a second response only once per designated item	Yes	No
14. Records 0, 1, or 2 points, as appropriate	Yes	No
15. Discontinues after four consecutive failures	Yes	No
16. Adds points correctly	Yes	No

Comments: _____

_____

_____

Symbol Search

Circle One

1. Reads directions verbatim	Yes	No
2. Reads directions clearly	Yes	No
3. Provides two No. 2 graphite pencils without erasers	Yes	No

Exhibit N-2 (*Continued*)

4. Points from examinee's left to right when giving instructions for sample item 1	Yes	No
5. Gives proper instructions for sample items 2 and 3	Yes	No
6. Offers praise such as "Good" or "Right" when examinee marks the correct answer for the three practice items	Yes	No
7. Gives correct instructions when examinee fails a practice item	Yes	No
8. Proceeds with test items only when examinee understands the task	Yes	No
9. Opens the Response Booklet to expose the first two pages of the subtest after examinee completes the practice items	Yes	No
10. Points to correct part of booklet as instructions are read for subtest items	Yes	No
11. Turns page briefly to show examinee third and fourth pages of items	Yes	No
12. Begins timing after completing instructions	Yes	No
13. Reminds examinee, if needed, to go in order and to continue the task until told to stop	Yes	No
14. Discontinues after 120 seconds	Yes	No
15. Places a mark through each correct item	Yes	No
16. Records number of correct and incorrect items accurately	Yes	No
17. Obtains score by subtracting number of incorrect from number of correct items	Yes	No

Comments: _____

_____

_____

Letter–Number Sequencing   *Circle One*

1. Reads directions verbatim	Yes	No
2. Reads directions clearly	Yes	No
3. Administers all five practice items	Yes	No
4. Corrects examinee if she or he makes an error on any practice item, and repeats instructions as necessary	Yes	No
5. Proceeds with the subtest even if examinee fails all practice items	Yes	No
6. Administers item 1 after practice items	Yes	No
7. Pronounces digits and letters singly, distinctly, at the rate of one number or letter per second, without chunking	Yes	No
8. Records examinee's response to each trial verbatim	Yes	No
9. Gives all three trials of each item	Yes	No
10. Pauses after each sequence to allow examinee to respond	Yes	No

11. Assigns 1 point for each trial passed	Yes	No
12. As long as numbers and letters are recalled in sequence, gives credit if the letters are recalled in sequence before the numbers	Yes	No
13. Discontinues after all three trials of an item are failed	Yes	No
14. Adds points correctly	Yes	No

Comments: _____

_____

_____

Object Assembly   *Circle One*

1. Reads directions verbatim	Yes	No
2. Reads directions clearly	Yes	No
3. Begins with item 1	Yes	No
4. Uses shield correctly	Yes	No
5. Presents puzzles with pieces arranged properly	Yes	No
6. Demonstrates correct arrangement on item 1 (man) if examinee's assembly is incorrect	Yes	No
7. Does not demonstrate correct arrangement on items 2–5, even if examinee's arrangements are incomplete or incorrect	Yes	No
8. Administers all items	Yes	No
9. Begins timing immediately after the last word of instructions	Yes	No
10. Stops timing when examinee is obviously finished	Yes	No
11. Allows examinee to continue working on a puzzle after time limit when examinee is nearing completion	Yes	No
12. If examinee turns over a piece, promptly and unobtrusively turns it right side up	Yes	No
13. Records time accurately	Yes	No
14. Records number of junctures correctly completed within time limit	Yes	No
15. Assigns no credit for correct responses given after time limit	Yes	No
16. Records points appropriately and accurately	Yes	No
17. Assigns proper time-bonus credit	Yes	No
18. Adds points correctly	Yes	No

Comments: _____

_____

_____

Exhibit N-2 (Continued)

Digit Symbol—Copy	Circle One	
1. Reads directions verbatim	Yes	No
2. Reads directions clearly	Yes	No
3. Provides two No. 2 graphite pencils without erasers	Yes	No
4. Provides a smooth work surface	Yes	No
5. Demonstrates by copying the first three symbols into the empty boxes	Yes	No
6. Corrects examinee's mistakes on sample items	Yes	No
7. Avoids timing sample items	Yes	No
8. Begins timing immediately after completing instructions	Yes	No
9. Records time accurately	Yes	No
10. Discontinues after 90 seconds	Yes	No
11. Records correct number of items	Yes	No
12. Avoids giving credit to sample items, incorrectly drawn items, or items completed out of sequence	Yes	No

Comments: _____

_____

_____

Other Aspects of Test Administration	Circle One	
1. Establishes rapport before testing	Yes	No
2. Encourages effort and offers appropriate feedback	Yes	No
3. Is well organized	Yes	No
4. Has needed material in kit	Yes	No
5. Has extra paper and pencils	Yes	No
6. Adheres to standardized instructions	Yes	No
7. Is fluid with the administration of the test	Yes	No
8. Has test materials and protocol out of examinee's view	Yes	No
9. Makes smooth transition from subtest to subtest	Yes	No
10. Provides support between subtests, as needed	Yes	No
11. Focuses examinee's attention on tasks	Yes	No
12. Takes breaks when appropriate (if needed)	Yes	No
13. Handles minor levels of anxiety and other behavior problems appropriately	Yes	No
14. Makes the test experience positive	Yes	No

Comments: _____

_____

_____

Score Conversion Page of Record Form	Circle One	
1. Transfers raw scores to Score Conversion Page for each subtest correctly	Yes	No
2. Converts raw scores to scaled scores for each subtest correctly	Yes	No
3. Adds scaled scores accurately for Verbal Scale	Yes	No
4. Adds scaled scores accurately for Performance Scale	Yes	No
5. Adds scaled scores accurately for Full Scale	Yes	No
6. Adds scaled scores accurately for Verbal Comprehension Index	Yes	No
7. Adds scaled scores accurately for Perceptual Organization Index	Yes	No
8. Adds scaled scores accurately for Working Memory Index	Yes	No
9. Adds scaled scores accurately for Processing Speed Index	Yes	No
10. Determines subtest strengths and weaknesses correctly	Yes	No
11. Completes Optional Procedures box for Digit Symbol—Incidental Learning and Digit Symbol—Copy correctly	Yes	No

Comments: _____

_____

_____

Profile Page	Circle One	
1. Transfers sums of scaled scores for IQs and Indexes to Profile Page correctly	Yes	No
2. Converts sum of scaled scores in Verbal Scale to IQ correctly	Yes	No
3. Converts sum of scaled scores in Performance Scale to IQ correctly	Yes	No
4. Converts sum of scaled scores in Full Scale to IQ correctly	Yes	No
5. Converts sum of scaled scores in Verbal Comprehension Index to Deviation IQ correctly	Yes	No
6. Converts sum of scaled scores in Perceptual Organization Index to Deviation IQ correctly	Yes	No
7. Converts sum of scaled scores in Working Memory Index to Deviation IQ correctly	Yes	No
8. Converts sum of scaled scores in Processing Speed Index to Deviation IQ correctly	Yes	No
9. Enters percentiles and confidence intervals for IQs and Indexes correctly	Yes	No

(Continued)

Exhibit N-2 (Continued)

10. Completes profile of subtest scores correctly   Yes   No
11. Completes profile of IQ scores correctly   Yes   No
12. Completes profile of Index scores correctly   Yes   No

Comments: _____

_____

_____

Discrepancy Analysis Page	Circle One	
1. Enters IQs and Index scores correctly	Yes	No
2. Calculates difference scores correctly	Yes	No
3. Enters selected significance level	Yes	No
4. Enters frequency of difference in standardization sample data for each discrepancy comparison correctly and divides each tabled frequency by 2	Yes	No
5. Enters longest Digit Span Forward correctly	Yes	No
6. Enters longest Digit Span Backward correctly	Yes	No
7. Calculates difference between Digits Forward and Digits Backward correctly	Yes	No

Comments: _____

_____

_____

Demographics Page	Circle One	
1. Completes identifying information section correctly: assumes that all months have 30 days for purposes of calculating chronological age; does not round up age (for example, 64 years 4 months 28 days is rounded to 64 years 4 months)	Yes	No

2. Completes behavioral observation section and under "Other Notes" records the examinee's race and occupation; if the examinee is retired, records the preretirement occupation   Yes   No
3. Writes examinee's name, the date, and examiner's name on Symbol Search Response Booklet, if subtest is given; circles whether the examinee is right or left handed   Yes   No

Comments: _____

_____

_____

Overall Evaluation of Test Administration

Circle One: Excellent   Good   Average   Poor   Failing

Qualitative feedback: _____

_____

_____

Overall strengths: _____

_____

_____

Areas of needed improvement: _____

_____

_____

Other comments: _____

_____

_____

administer the Block Design subtest to an examinee with impaired language comprehension, begin with item 5. Place four blocks in front of him or her, and turn each block to show the different sides while pointing in a manner that focuses the examinee's attention on the different colors. Next, arrange the blocks into design 5 and give the examinee four additional blocks. Then point to the examinee, point to the blocks, and point to the completed model. If the examinee fails an item or does not respond, assemble his or her blocks to match the design and then point first to the examinee's blocks and then to the model. Then scramble the examinee's blocks, point to the examinee, point to the scrambled blocks, and point to the model.

Visual functions. You will need to determine whether the examinee has adequate visual ability to be administered the nonverbal subtests. In all cases, review the referral material, health history, and recent medical findings. Before formal testing, you can screen for visual acuity by having the examinee read a brief paragraph (if the examinee should be able to read) or describe pictures (if the examinee is a poor reader). It is always good practice to ask the examinee whether she or he wears glasses and is colorblind before you begin testing. It also is good practice to ask the examinee whether she or he can see the designs and numbers clearly when you introduce the Digit Symbol—Coding and Symbol Search subtests during standard administration.

In addition to visual acuity problems, be alert for deficits in primary visual perception or visual scanning, especially if the examinee has a history of stroke or degenerative brain disease. For example, completely misidentifying the Picture Completion items may suggest visual agnosia, whereas consistent failure to use all of the Picture Arrangement cards may reflect inattention to one side of space. When an examinee has a visual perceptual problem, the standard WAIS–III administration procedures may not be appropriate.

Kaplan, Fein, Morris, and Delis (1991) provide useful strategies for administering WAIS–III subtests to individuals with visual perceptual or visual scanning difficulties. For example, when you administer Picture Completion to an examinee with impaired visual acuity, you might place a sheet magnifier directly over the individual items as you present them. Or, when you administer Picture Arrangement to an examinee with left-sided visual neglect, you can place the cards vertically in the examinee's intact visual field and instruct him or her to arrange the cards from top to bottom. Although these changes modify the standard procedure and may make use of the norms questionable, they appear to be relatively minor modifications. Still, it would be helpful to have research about the effects of test procedure modifications on WAIS–III scores.

Obviously, it is inappropriate to administer the WAIS–III Performance Scale to severely visually impaired examinees. However, you can administer the Verbal subtests to estimate their language-based cognitive functioning. The only necessary modification of standard instructions involves the Comprehension subtest. To avoid confusion, instruct examinees (where needed) to answer items 4 and 12 as if they were fully sighted (Shindell, 1989).

Motor functions. Some types of motor problems may affect examinees' performance on the WAIS–III. These include (a) motor slowing, (b) arthritis in the fingers and hands, (c) dystonic disorders (involuntary, abnormal postures or spasms of the muscles of the head, neck, trunk, or extremities that are painful and interfere with the examinee's ability to engage in voluntary movements), (d) postural tremors (tremors that occur when muscles are activated and the limbs are maintained in certain positions, such as when the arms are held outstretched; the tremors are absent when the limbs are relaxed), (e) intention tremors (tremors that interfere with voluntary movements; the tremors are absent when the examinee is inactive, but when she or he attempts to perform exacting, precise movements, the affected limb begins to oscillate, making the precise movement difficult or impossible to execute), and (f) medication-induced motor impairment. Motor problems may be present in hemiplegia and progressive movement disorders such as Parkinson's disease.

In most cases, you can evaluate the verbal-comprehension cognitive ability of examinees with severe motor difficulties by administering the WAIS–III Verbal subtests. Hemiplegic individuals who have an intact dominant upper extremity can be evaluated with both Verbal and Performance subtests. For those who have an intact nondominant hand only, omit the Digit Symbol—Coding and Symbol Search subtests, but attempt to administer the remaining subtests.

Subtest Sequence

Administer the subtests in the order specified in the manual unless you have a compelling reason to use another order. In the case of an examinee who is extremely bored or frustrated, a compelling reason might be to give a different subtest or a subtest of the examinee's choice to motivate her or him. Or, only selected subtests might be given to an examinee with a sensory handicap, as noted above. Another compelling reason for adjusting the order of administration would be to accommodate examinees who fatigue easily (e.g., those who are physically ill or elderly) or display marked anxiety about the testing situation. Examinees who fatigue easily may be given subtests such as Digit Span, Arithmetic, Digit Symbol—Coding, or Symbol Search early in the session, when their energy levels and attention-concentration skills may be best. Anxious examinees may be started with subtests that are relatively nonthreatening and do not have strict time limits (e.g., Information, Comprehension, or Vocabulary). However, examinees with test anxiety are likely to feel anxious when they begin the test, regardless of which subtest is given first.

Using the standard sequence of administration provides you with a baseline for evaluating examinees whom you will test in the future; it also ensures that the order you use is comparable to that used by other examiners. Following the order specified in the WAIS–III manual, which alternates nonverbal and verbal subtests, also may help to maintain the examinee's interest in the tasks.

If you elect to administer 13 subtests, simply omit Object Assembly. If you give the 11 standard subtests and omit Letter–Number Sequencing, Symbol Search, and Object Assembly, follow the order presented in Table 3.2 on page 37 in the *WAIS–III Administration and Scoring Manual*.

The *WAIS–III Administration and Scoring Manual* states that "Picture Completion was moved to the initial position in the sequence because it provides a colorful, nonverbal introduction to the scale, which should help the examinee 'warm up' to the testing situation" (p. 36). However, for examinees who have difficulty with perceptual discrimination or who respond slowly, Picture Completion may actually induce frustration and reduce motivation to continue with the test. Therefore, carefully attend to the examinee's behavior, especially at the beginning of the test session. Do not assume that the new order of the subtests will automatically reduce every examinee's anxiety level or help him or her to feel relaxed. We need research to learn about how the order in which the subtests are administered affects examinees' anxiety level and test performance.

Some examinees—such as those who are depressed and work slowly or those with a neurological disorder or psychiatric disorder—may not be able to complete the test in a single session. In such cases, schedule breaks to coincide with the end of a subtest so that testing can easily be resumed at a later time. In the rare instances when a subtest must be interrupted prior to completion, resume administration of the subtest where you stopped, except on Similarities, Block Design, Matrix Reasoning, and Picture Arrangement. On these subtests, the easy items provide some examinees with the practice they need to succeed at more difficult items. Therefore, it is best that you complete these subtests before you stop the session. However, if you must interrupt one of these sub-

tests, readminister the first few items at the next session so that the examinee can establish a mental set that may help her or him succeed on the harder items. Naturally, changes in standard administration procedures may affect the validity of the test, but minor changes do not appear to be critical.

Starting Rules

Six of the 14 subtests begin with the first item (Digit Span, Letter–Number Sequencing, Digit Symbol—Coding, Picture Arrangement, Symbol Search, and Object Assembly). Of the remaining eight subtests, three begin with the fourth item (Vocabulary, Comprehension, and Matrix Reasoning), three begin with the fifth item (Information, Arithmetic, and Block Design), and two begin with the sixth item (Picture Completion and Similarities). If the examinee obtains maximum scores on the first two subtest items administered, which are designated as *basal items*, assign him or her credit for the items that precede the basal items, even though these items were not given. If the examinee does not obtain maximum credit on *both* of the basal items, administer the preceding items in reverse sequence until he or she obtains maximum scores on two consecutive items. If the examinee obtained maximum credit on the starting item, count it as a success in the reverse sequence.

Occasionally, you may have doubts about whether the examinee passed both basal items. When this happens, you will need to administer earlier items in the subtest. The *WAIS–III Administration and Scoring Manual* does not provide guidance on how to credit items that the examinee fails *below* the starting point. We recommend the following starting-point scoring rule: *If subsequent scoring of the items indicates that the early items were administered unnecessarily, give the examinee full credit for these items even if she or he earned only partial or no credit.* In other words, if the examinee fails (or receives only partial credit for) one or more items below the starting point but further checking indicates that, in fact, the examinee correctly answered the items at the starting point, give full credit for those items that precede the basal items. This starting-point scoring rule favors the examinee by ensuring that she or he is not penalized for failing items that should not have been administered in the first place. The starting-point scoring rule also helps to maintain standardized scoring procedures.

Discontinuance Rules

Of the 14 subtests in the test, 11 have discontinuance rules; that is, these 11 subtests are discontinued after a specified number of consecutive items are failed. The three subtests without discontinuance rules are Object Assembly, Digit Symbol—Coding, and Symbol Search. On the 11 subtests with discontinuance rules, you will need to administer additional items until you are certain the discontinuance criterion has been met. If you administer additional items in a subtest because you are not sure whether the items at the discontinuance point were failed, use the following discontinuance-point scoring rule to determine how to credit the additional items (Wechsler, 1997): *If subsequent scoring of the items indicates that the additional items were administered unnecessarily, do not give the examinee credit for items that he or she passed after the discontinuance point.* This scoring rule prevents the examinee from receiving credit for items that did not need to be administered. This rule constitutes an attempt to maintain standardized scoring procedures.

Repetition of Items

Use judgment in deciding when to repeat questions. However, you *cannot* repeat the Digit Span or Letter–Number Sequencing items.

Use of Probing Questions and Queries

Use probing questions when responses are ambiguous, vague, or incomplete or when probing is indicated by a (Q) in the scoring section of the *WAIS–III Administration and Scoring Manual.* When a response is followed by a (Q), the examinee must give the response shown after the (Q) in order to get the appropriate credit. Thus, the entire response—the initial answer plus the response to the query—is used in determining the appropriate credit.

Spoiled Responses

An explicit scoring rule on the WAIS–III is that you give a score of 0 to a spoiled response (see pp. 48–49, *WAIS–III Administration and Scoring Manual*). A spoiled response is one that initially was partially correct but was spoiled by the examinee's incorrect elaboration on his or her initial response. For example, let's suppose an examinee defines *summer* as "one of the seasons." This is a 1-point answer. In response to a probe, however, he or she replies "the cold time of year." This elaboration reveals the examinee's misconception about the meaning of *summer,* and the response receives a score of 0.

Modifying Standard Procedures

Use modifications in test administration designed for testing-of-limits (see Chapter 5) only *after* the entire WAIS–III has been administered according to standard procedures. Modifications may be helpful in clinical assessment, but they may invalidate the scores if they are used during the standard administration.

How to Proceed When a Basal Level Is Not Established

The *WAIS–III Administration and Scoring Manual* (first printing) does not provide directions for continuing or discontinuing a subtest when a basal level is not established. The subtests that require a basal level—that is, perfect scores on two consecutive items—are Picture Completion, Vocabulary, Similarities, Block Design, Arithmetic, Matrix Reasoning, Information, and Comprehension. There are many possible cases in which a basal level will not be established. The following three examples illustrate failure to establish a basal level (that is, 2-point responses on two consecutive items) on the Vocabulary subtest: (a) An examinee earns 1 point on item 5, 2 points on item 4, 0 points on item 3, 2 points on item 2, and 1 point on item 1. (b) Another examinee earns 1 point on item 5, 1 point on item 4, 1 point on item 3, 0 points on item 2, and 2 points on item 1. (c) A third examinee earns 1 point on each of the first five items.

In any situation in which a basal level is not established, we recommend that the discontinuance procedure be followed for the subtest. (David Tulsky of The Psychological Corporation fully supports this recommendation; personal communication, May 1998.) This recommendation means that it is not necessary to establish a basal level in order to continue with a subtest. The basal criterion, however, is important for deciding whether to administer the items in a subtest in reverse order. Maintaining standard procedures is critical if all examinees are to be given the same opportunities to demonstrate their competencies. Further, when all examiners follow the same test procedures, users of the test can have more confidence in the results obtained by different examiners.

SHORT FORMS OF THE WAIS–III

It takes approximately 75 minutes, with a range of 60 to 90 minutes, to administer the 11 standard WAIS–III subtests (Wechsler, 1997). These time estimates are based on normal individuals in the standardization sample and may not generalize to clinical populations. In fact, there are data indicating that, in a clinic sample, the administration time for the 11 standard WAIS–III subtests is usually longer than that reported for a normal sample—mean of 91.24 minutes, with a range of 54.43 minutes to 136.01 minutes (Ryan, Werth, & Lopez, 1998). This study also reported that administration time for 13 subtests was about 8 minutes longer on the average—mean of 99.48 minutes, with a range of 61.29 minutes to 144.00 minutes.

When time is at a premium, you can use short forms of the WAIS–III as *screening devices* (when administration of the short form may be followed by administration of the remaining subtests), *for research purposes* (to describe the intellectual level of a group), and *for a quick check on an individual's intellectual status* (and only when the IQ is peripheral to the referral question) (Silverstein, 1990b). Ideally, you should select a short form based on such criteria as acceptable reliability and validity, the ability of the short form to answer the referral question and provide clinically useful information, the examinee's physical capabilities, and the amount of time available for test administration. Short forms of the WAIS–III have the same advantages and disadvantages as do short forms of the WISC–III. Chapter 6 discusses the use of short forms; review this material as needed. Let's now consider different WAIS–III short forms.

Selecting the Short Form

Table O-6 in Appendix O provides the 10 best short-form combinations of two, three, four, and five WAIS–III subtests and also shows other short forms designed to optimize time and scoring and designed for use with hard-of-hearing individuals. The reliability and validity coefficients shown in Table O-6 were calculated using the standardization data and the Tellegen and Briggs (1967) procedure, which takes into account the reliabilities of the subtests used in the short form. Exhibit I-4 in Appendix I (pages 1069–1070) shows the formulas used to compute the reliability and validity of the short-form combinations.

An inspection of the coefficients in Table O-6 indicates that the 10 best two-, three-, four-, and five-subtest short-form combinations all have reliability coefficients of .90 or higher. In fact, all four- and five-subtest combinations have reliability coefficients of .94 or higher. Overall, for the combinations shown in Table O-6, the more subtests used in a short form, the higher will be the reliability of the estimated IQ.

It is also helpful to consider the validity of the short-form combinations. The validity coefficients are .90 or higher for all four- and five-subtest short forms shown in Table O-6. For the three-subtest short-form combinations, 8 out of the 10 best combinations have validity coefficients of .90, and the other two are .899. Finally, the validity coefficients for the 10 best two-subtest short-form combinations range from .853 to .881. The best two-, three-, four-, and five-subtest short-form combinations, based on validity and reliability, are as follows: (a) Vocabulary and Matrix Reasoning, (b) Vocabulary, Information, and Block Design, (c) Vocabulary, Information, Block Design, and Matrix Reasoning, and (d) Vocabulary, Arithmetic, Information, Picture Completion, and Matrix Reasoning. The subtests in the best two-, three-, and four-subtest combinations also are excellent measures of *g*.

You also want to consider the short-form combinations that you can use for a rapid screening, taking into account the purpose of the screening and the physical capacities of the examinee. We believe that the following subtests take the least time and are the easiest to score: Arithmetic, Digit Span, Information, Letter–Number Sequencing, Picture Completion, Digit Symbol—Coding, Matrix Reasoning, and Symbol Search. For these eight subtests, the short-form combinations (a) Information and Matrix Reasoning and (b) Arithmetic, Information, and Matrix Reasoning represent good measures of *g*, whereas the short-form combinations (c) Arithmetic, Information, Picture Completion, and Matrix Reasoning and (d) Arithmetic, Information, Picture Completion,

Digit Symbol—Coding, and Matrix Reasoning have subtests that are either good or fair measures of *g*.

Because many of the short forms of the WAIS–III have high reliability and validity, clinical considerations also should guide you in selecting a short form. For instance, if you want to use a four-subtest short form, consider selecting a combination of two Verbal and two Performance Scale subtests, to obtain some representation of both verbal and performance skills in your screening.

Sometimes you may want to use a short form to screen for some specific type of problem, such as a memory problem (Arithmetic, Digit Span, and Letter–Number Sequencing) or a visual-motor speed problem (Digit Symbol—Coding and Symbol Search). In these cases, you should not use the estimated Deviation IQ obtained on the specialized short form as a measure of intelligence, because the specialized short form may lead to an underestimate of the examinee's IQ if you have prior evidence that the examinee has a possible weakness. Instead, we recommend that you administer a short form that does not include the subtests in question to derive an estimated IQ. This procedure allows you to screen for IQ, screen for a particular problem, and screen for the difference between the two short-form measures.

An examinee's physical capabilities also may guide you in selecting a short form. Examinees with marked visual impairment or severe motor dysfunction of the upper extremities, as you have read, will have difficulty with the Performance Scale subtests. In these cases, the Verbal Scale (or subtests that form the Verbal Comprehension Index score) serves as a useful short form. For hearing-impaired examinees, the Performance Scale (or subtests that form the Perceptual Organization Index score) is a useful short form. Administer these short forms by using the examinee's preferred mode of communication and, if possible, supplement your evaluation by using other tests designed to accommodate the special physical abilities of the examinee.

After the short form has been given, you will need to convert the scaled scores to an estimated Deviation IQ. Tables O-7 through O-11 in Appendix O provide the estimated Deviation IQs for short-form combinations of two, three, four, five, six, and seven subtests that (a) have the best validity, (b) can be administered and scored rapidly, (c) can be given to hard-of-

hearing individuals, and (d) can be used to obtain Index scores. If the short form you select is not in Table O-6, then follow the procedures outlined in Exhibit I-4 in Appendix I (pages 1069–1070) to convert the composite scores to Deviation Quotients. Use Table C-36 in Appendix C (page 850) to obtain the appropriate *a* and *b* constants. To obtain r_{jk}, use the section of Table A.1 (pp. 218–230, *WAIS–III—WMS–III Technical Manual*) that corresponds to the examinee's age group.

The estimated Deviation Quotients shown in Appendix O for the short forms that comprise the four Index scores differ somewhat from those shown in the *WAIS–III Administration and Scoring Manual*. The Psychological Corporation constructed its norms by using a *z* score conversion of the scaled scores, transforming the scores to a distribution with $M = 100$ and $SD = 15$ and then smoothing out irregularities in the distribution (personal communication, David Tulsky of The Psychological Corporation, May 1998). The Tellegen and Briggs (1967) procedure uses a linear transformation of the scaled scores without smoothing. Research with a clinical sample of 74 individuals indicated that the two methods produced mean Deviation Quotients that were essentially identical (Sattler & Ryan, 1998). In addition, the two methods produced Index scores that were within 1 point of each other in 95 percent or more of the cases. Finally, correlations between the Index scores generated by the two methods ranged from .965 to .999. We recommend that you use The Psychological Corporation values on pages 199 to 202 of the manual. However, if you wish to compare the four Index short forms with other short forms proposed in this text, then the Deviation IQs shown in Appendix O might be more appropriate.

Satz-Mogel Abbreviated Procedure

The Yudin short form procedure, which reduces the number of items within subtests, is known as the Satz-Mogel short form when applied to the WAIS–III (Satz & Mogel, 1962). Research with the WAIS–R indicates that this procedure provides IQs with high validity coefficients (Silverstein, 1985). However, poor correlations have been reported between estimated subtest scaled scores and actually obtained scores (Evans, 1985). Estimated scaled scores have been found to exceed the range of +2 scaled-score points from actually obtained scores in over 25 percent of 81 cases studied (Evans, 1985). Additionally, when the Satz-Mogel procedure is used, some or all of the subtest scores show relatively poor reliability and stability (Paolo & Ryan, 1993; Silverstein, 1990a; 1990b), rendering the data unsuitable for profile analysis (Mattis, Hanny & Meyers, 1992).

An important limitation of the Satz-Mogel short form is that it is inappropriate to use as a screening device. It is difficult to imagine a situation in which administration of a Satz-Mogel short form would be followed by administration of the remaining items in the original scale. However, a short form that uses all of the items in selected subtests can be useful as a screening instrument and, if needed, be followed by other subtests.

Finally, as noted in Appendix I, a major problem with reduced-item short forms that researchers have not addressed is that they represent a radical departure from the standard administration (personal communication, Leslie Atkinson, January 1992). When half of the items in a subtest are excluded, the difficulty slope of the items increases much more rapidly than when all appropriate items are given, and the opportunity for practice decreases equally rapidly. Research usually involves administering the entire scale and generating validity coefficients for the relevant half. This situation is different from simply administering half of the items. For these reasons, Atkinson recommended that we not use reduced-item short forms such as those proposed by Satz and Mogel and by Yudin. Therefore, we are not including the specific procedures for obtaining this WAIS–III short form in this text.

Two Two-Subtest Short-Form Combinations

A two-subtest combination that is popular as a short-form screening instrument is Vocabulary plus Block Design. These two subtests have moderate correlations with the Full Scale, have consistently high reliabilities, and are good measures of g. If this combination is chosen, Table O-7 in Appendix O can be used to convert the sum of scaled scores directly into an estimated Full Scale IQ. The reliability of the composite is high ($r_{xx} = .93$ for the average of the 13 age groups in the standardization sample).

Another useful two-subtest short form is Vocabulary plus Matrix Reasoning. These two subtests also have moderate correlations with the Full Scale, have consistently high reliabilities, and are good measures of g. If this combination is chosen, Table O-7 in Appendix O can be used to convert the sum of scaled scores directly into an estimated Full Scale IQ. The reliability of the composite is high ($r_{xx} = .94$ for the average of the 13 age groups in the standardization sample).

Two Four-Subtest Short-Form Combinations

Two excellent four-subtest short forms are (a) Information, Arithmetic, Picture Completion, and Block Design and (b) Information, Arithmetic, Picture Completion, and Matrix Reasoning. Both of these combinations contain two Verbal subtests and two Performance subtests. They both have high reliability ($r_{xx} = .95$ for the average of the 13 age groups in the standardization sample). Both of these short forms take longer to administer than the Vocabulary and Block Design short form or the Vocabulary and Matrix Reasoning short form, but they provide more clinical and diagnostic information (e.g., additional information about concentration and attention). You can use Table O-9 in Appendix O to convert the sum of scaled scores on these two four-subtest short forms directly into an estimated Deviation Quotient. You also can use these short forms to obtain estimated Deviation IQs for the Verbal Scale (Information and Arithmetic) and Performance Scales (e.g., Picture Completion and Block Design) (see Table O-7). The Information, Arithmetic, Picture Completion, and Matrix Reasoning combination requires less time to administer than the Information, Arithmetic, Picture Completion, and Block Design combination. Table O-9 shows other excellent four-subtest short-form combinations.

One Six-Subtest Short-Form Combination

A six-subtest short-form combination that consists of Vocabulary, Similarities, Information, Picture Completion, Block Design, and Matrix Reasoning is useful to obtain the Verbal Comprehension Index score (Vocabulary, Similarities, and Information), the Perceptual Organization Index score (Picture Completion, Block Design, and Matrix Reasoning), and an estimated Deviation Quotient for the entire scale. You can use Table O-11 in Appendix O to convert the sums of scaled scores on these six subtests into an estimated Deviation Quotient. Table O-8 in Appendix O provides the Deviation Quotients for the Verbal Comprehension Index score and the Perceptual Organization Index score.

Two Seven-Subtest Short-Form Combinations

One potentially useful seven-subtest short-form combination is Information, Arithmetic, Digit Span, Similarities, Picture Completion, Block Design, and Digit Symbol—Coding (Ward, 1990). Research with the WAIS–R indicated that this short form reduces administration time by approximately 50 percent (Ryan & Rosenberg, 1984); provides estimates of the Verbal, Performance, and Full Scale IQs; and possesses excellent reliability (Axelrod, Woodard, Schretlen, & Benedict, 1996). This short form in the WAIS–III has a reliability coefficient of .96 for the average of the 13 age groups in the standardization sample. Additionally, this short form has performed well both as a screening instrument and as a substitute for the standard WAIS–R in normal and clinical samples (Paolo & Ryan, 1992; Paolo, Ryan, Ward, & Hilmer, 1996; Ryan, Abraham, Axelrod, & Paolo, 1996). Table O-11 in Appendix O can be used to convert the sums of the scaled scores on these seven subtests into an estimated Full Scale IQ. To obtain an estimated Deviation IQ for the Verbal and Performance Scales, consult Table O-9 for the Verbal Scale (four subtests) and Table O-8 for the Performance Scale (three subtests).

Another potentially useful seven-subtest short-form combination is Information, Arithmetic, Digit Span, Similarities, Picture Completion, Matrix Reasoning, and Digit Symbol—Coding. This combination also has a reliability coefficient of .96 for the average of the 13 age groups in the standardization sample. Table O-11 in Appendix O can be used to convert the sum of the scaled scores on these seven subtests into an estimated Full Scale IQ. To obtain an estimated Deviation IQ for the Verbal and Per-

formance Scales, consult Table O-9 for the Verbal Scale (four subtests) and Table O-8 for the Performance Scale (three subtests).

CHOOSING BETWEEN THE WAIS–III AND THE WISC–III

The WAIS–III overlaps with the WISC–III for ages 16-0-0 to 16-11-30. The overlap in ages between the WAIS–III and the WISC–III is especially helpful in retest situations. For example, an adolescent first administered the WAIS–III at 16 years of age can be retested with the WISC–III at any time during the next 11 months. In the overlapping ranges, Atkinson (personal communication, April 1998) compared the WAIS–III and the WISC–III on several criteria, including mean subtest reliability, Full Scale reliability, mean subtest floor, mean subtest ceiling, item gradients (refers to the number of items needed to go from the floor to the mean and from the mean to the ceiling and the relationship of raw-score points to scaled-score points), Full Scale floor, and Full Scale ceiling. He makes the following recommendations:

- *The WISC–III is a better choice for adolescents with below-average ability.*

- *Either test is adequate for adolescents with average ability.*

- *The WAIS–III is a better choice for adolescents with above-average ability.*

The following example illustrates how you can obtain a more thorough sampling on the WISC–III than on the WAIS–III for a 16-year-, 8-month-old adolescent with below-average ability. On Information, to obtain a scaled score of 5, the adolescent needs a raw score of 14 on the WISC–III but a raw score of only 5 on the WAIS–III.

The previous recommendations were based on internal psychometric data. The issue of validity still needs to be addressed. In the final analysis, the choice of a test in the overlapping ages should depend on the validity of the inferences that you can make from the scores on it. To this end, validity studies that compare the WAIS–III with the WISC–III in their overlapping age ranges, using samples of both normal and exceptional adolescents, would be helpful.

WAIS–III SUBTESTS

Vocabulary

The Vocabulary subtest contains 33 words arranged in order of increasing difficulty. Each word is presented orally and in print, and the examinee is asked to explain its meaning aloud. Responses are scored 2, 1, or 0. All examinees begin with the fourth word. If the examinee earns 2-point scores on both items 4 and 5, assign full credit for items 1, 2, and 3. If the examinee earns a score of 0 or 1 on either item 4 or item 5, administer items 1, 2, and 3 in *reverse sequence* until the examinee has two consecutive perfect scores. The subtest is discontinued after six consecutive failures.

Rationale. The rationale presented for the WISC–III Vocabulary subtest also applies to the WAIS–III Vocabulary subtest (see Appendix J, page 1086).

Factor analytic findings. The Vocabulary subtest is the best measure of g in the scale (69 percent of its variance may be attributed to g). This subtest contributes substantially to the Verbal Comprehension factor (Average loading = .91). Specificity is either ample or adequate for 11 age groups (16–17, 18–19, 20–24, 30–34, 35–44, 45–54, 55–64, 70–74, 75–79, 80–84, 85–89 years); at two age groups (25–29, 65–69 years) it is inadequate.

Reliability and correlational highlights. Vocabulary is the most reliable subtest in the scale (r_{xx} = .93), with reliability coefficients at or above .90 in each of the 13 age groups (range of .90 to .95). It correlates better with Information (r = .77) than with any other subtests. It has a high correlation with the Full Scale (r = .80) and the Verbal Scale (r = .83) and a moderately high correlation with the Performance Scale (r = .65).

Administrative and interpretive considerations. The administrative and interpretive considerations presented for the WISC–III Vocabulary subtest generally apply to the WAIS–III (see Appendix J, pages 1086–1087). On the WAIS–III Vocabulary subtest, however, the examinee looks at each word as the examiner pronounces it. Also, when the examinee gives a 0- or 1-point definition on the first basal word (i.e., item 4), you do not give him or her any help.

Study carefully the Sample Responses presented in the *WAIS–III Administration and Scoring Manual* so that you will know which responses require further inquiry, indicated by (Q). The examples indicate that many 0- and 1-point responses should be queried. When a 2-point response is accompanied by a (Q), it is the entire response including the elaboration that is worth 2 points.

Similarities

The Similarities subtest contains 19 pairs of words; the examinee is asked to explain the similarity between the two words in each pair. All examinees begin with the sixth word pair. If the examinee obtains 2-point scores on both items 6 and 7, assign full credit for items 1 through 5. If the examinee receives a score of 0 or 1 on either item 6 or item 7, administer items 1 through 5 in *reverse order* until the examinee has two consecutive perfect scores. Items 1 through 5 are scored 0 or 1; items 6 through 19 are scored 2, 1, or 0, depending on the conceptual level of the response. The subtest is discontinued after four consecutive failures.

Rationale. The rationale described for the WISC–III Similarities subtest also applies to the WAIS–III Similarities subtest (see Appendix J, page 1082).

Factor analytic findings. Similarities is tied with Information as the second best measure of g in the scale (62 percent of its variance may be attributed to g). This subtest contributes substantially to the Verbal Comprehension factor (Average loading = .77). Specificity is either ample or adequate for eight age groups (16–17, 18–19, 25–29, 35–44, 45–54, 55–64, 80–84, 85–89 years); at five age groups (20–24, 30–34, 65–69, 70–74, 75–79 years) it is inadequate.

Reliability and correlational highlights. Similarities is a reliable subtest (r_{xx} = .86), with reliability coefficients at or above .81 in each of the 13 age groups (range of .81 to .89). It correlates better with Vocabulary (r = .76), Information (r = .70), and Comprehension (r = .70) than with any of the other subtests. It has a moderately high correlation with the Full Scale (r = .76), the Verbal Scale (r = .77), and the Performance Scale (r = .65).

Administrative and interpretive considerations. Most of the administrative and interpretive considerations presented for the WISC–III Similarities subtest apply to the WAIS–III (see Appendix J, pages 1082–1083). The major difference is that on the WAIS–III the subtest starts with item 6. Considerable skill is required to score Similarities responses. Study carefully the sample responses that follow each item. These sample responses also list responses that you need to probe, shown by a (Q). Also, master the general scoring principles, which elucidate the rationale for 2, 1, and 0 scores (see p. 112, *WAIS–III Administration and Scoring Manual*).

Arithmetic

The Arithmetic subtest contains 20 items; 17 are given orally and the other three use blocks along with oral directions. All examinees begin with item 5. If the examinee gives correct responses (1-point answers) to both items 5 and 6, give the examinee full credit for items 1 through 4. If the examinee fails either item 5 or item 6, administer items 1 through 4 in *reverse sequence* until she or he obtains credit on two consecutive items. All problems are timed, with items 1 through 6 having a time limit of 15 seconds; items 7 through 11, 30 seconds; items 12 through 19, 60 seconds; and item 20, 120 seconds. All items are scored 1 or 0, with one additional time-bonus point possible on items 19 and 20. The subtest is discontinued after four consecutive failures.

Rationale. The rationale presented for the WISC–III Arithmetic subtest also applies to the WAIS–III Arithmetic subtest (see Appendix J, page 1084).

Factor analytic findings. Arithmetic is a good measure of g (56 percent of its variance may be attributed to g). This subtest contributes moderately to the Working Memory factor (Average loading = .50). Subtest specificity is either ample or adequate for all age groups.

Reliability and correlational highlights. Arithmetic is a reliable subtest (r_{xx} = .88), with reliability coefficients at or above .77 in each of the 13 age groups (range of .77 to .91). It correlates better with Information (r = .63) and Vocabulary (r = .60) than with any of the other subtests. It has a moderately high correlation with the Full Scale (r = .72), the Verbal Scale (r = .70), and the Performance Scale (r = .63).

Administrative and interpretive considerations. The administrative and interpretive considerations discussed for the WISC–III Arithmetic subtest generally apply to the WAIS–III (see Appendix J, pages 1084–1085). However, a booklet is not used to present any of the WAIS–III Arithmetic items to the examinee.

Digit Span

The Digit Span subtest has two parts: Digits Forward, which contains series of numbers ranging from two to nine digits in length, and Digits Backward, which contains series of numbers ranging from two to eight digits in length. The examinee listens to a series of digits given orally by the examiner and then repeats the digits. There are two sets of digits of each length. Digits Forward is administered first, followed by Digits Backward. All series are scored 2, 1, or 0. On both parts of the subtest, testing is discontinued after failure on both trials of any series. On the WAIS–III Digit Span is a regular subtest, whereas on the WISC–III it is a supplementary subtest.

The *WAIS–III Administration and Scoring Manual* does not provide separate scaled scores for Digits Forward and Digits Backward. However, there are two useful tables in this manual that show how the standardization sample performed on Digits Forward and on Digits Backward. Table B.6 (page 212 of the WAIS–III manual) shows the longest Digits Forward span and the longest Digits Backward span recalled by the standardization sample. Across all age groups, the standardization sample had a median Digits Forward span of 6 (range of 6 to 7) and a median Digits Backward span of 5 (range of 4 to 5) (see Table N-16).

Table B.7 (page 213 of the WAIS–III manual) shows the extent to which the standardization sample recalled more digits forward than backward and vice versa. In all age groups and in the total sample, the standardization sample recalled more digits forward than backward (*Mdn* difference = 2 points for all age groups). Thus, you can consider as noteworthy raw-score

Table N-16
Median Number of Digits Recalled on WAIS–III Digits Forward and Digits Backward, by Age Group

Age group	Median	
	Forward	Backward
16–17	7	5
18–19	7	5
20–24	7	5
25–29	7	5
30–34	7	5
35–44	7	5
45–54	6	4
55–64	6	4
65–69	6	4
70–74	6	4
75–79	6	4
80–84	6	4
85–89	6	4
Average	6	5

Source: Adapted from Wechsler (1997), Table B.6 (p. 212).

Table N-17
Percentage of Individuals in Standardization Group Who Recalled More WAIS–III Digits Backward than Digits Forward, by Age Group

Age group	Percent
16–17	4.0
18–19	5.0
20–24	2.0
25–29	5.0
30–34	4.5
35–44	5.0
45–54	1.5
55–64	5.0
65–69	4.0
70–74	3.0
75–79	4.0
80–84	3.3
85–89	2.0
Average	3.8

Source: Adapted from Wechsler (1997), Table B.7 (p. 213).

differences of 3 points (or more) between Digits Forward and Digits Backward. The percentage of the standardization sample who recalled more digits backward than forward was 3.8 percent for the total group (range of 1.5 to 5 percent in the 13 age groups) (see Table N-17).

Rationale. The rationale presented for the WISC–III Digit Span subtest also applies to the WAIS–III Digit Span subtest (see Appendix J, pages 1089–1090).

Factor analytic findings. The Digit Span subtest is a fair measure of g (32 percent of its variance may be attributed to g). This subtest contributes substantially to the Working Memory factor (Average loading = .67). Specificity is ample for all age groups.

Reliability and correlational highlights. Digit Span is a reliable subtest (r_{xx} = .90), with reliability coefficients at or above .84 in each of the 13 age groups (range of .84 to .93). It correlates better with Letter–Number Sequencing (r = .57) and Arithmetic (r = .52) than with any of the other subtests. It has a moderate correlation with the Full Scale (r = .52) and the Verbal Scale (r = .51) and a moderately low correlation with the Performance Scale (r = .47).

Administrative and interpretive considerations. The administrative and interpretive considerations presented for the WISC–III Digit Span subtest also are relevant for the WAIS–III (see Appendix J, pages 1090–1091).

Information

The Information subtest has 28 questions that sample a broad range of general knowledge about common events, objects, and places. Items dealing with historical and geographic facts also are included. Each item is scored 1 or 0 (pass-fail). All examinees begin with item 5. If an examinee obtains 1 point on questions 5 and 6, assign her or him full credit for items 1 through 4. If an examinee earns a score of 0 on either item 5 or item 6, administer items 1 through 4 in *reverse order* until the examinee passes two consecutive items. The subtest is discontinued after six consecutive failures. The questions can usually be answered with a simply stated fact. The examinee is not required to find relationships between facts in order to receive credit.

Rationale. The rationale presented for the WISC–III Information subtest applies to the WAIS–III Information subtest as well (see Appendix J, pages 1080–1081).

Factor analytic findings. Information is tied with Similarities as the second best measure of g in the scale (62 percent of its variance may be attributed to g). This subtest contributes substantially to the Verbal Comprehension factor (Average loading = .83). Specificity is ample or adequate for all age groups.

Reliability and correlational highlights. Information is a reliable subtest (r_{xx} = .91), with reliability coefficients at or above .89 in each of the 13 age groups (range of .89 to .93). It correlates better with Vocabulary (r = .77) than with any of the other subtests. It has a moderately high correlation with the Full Scale (r = .76), the Verbal Scale (r = .79), and the Performance Scale (r = .63).

Administrative and interpretive considerations. The administrative and interpretive considerations presented for the WISC–III Information subtest also are relevant for the WAIS–III (see Appendix J, pages 1081–1082).

Comprehension

The Comprehension subtest contains 18 questions covering a wide range of situations and proverbs. Questions deal with such issues as government operations and laws, health standards, and social mores. All examinees begin the subtest with item 4. If examinees give 2-point answers on both items 4 and 5, assign full credit for items 1 through 3.

Items 1 through 3 are scored 0 or 1; items 4 through 18 are scored 0, 1, or 2. If an examinee earns a score of 0 or 1 on either item 4 or item 5, administer items 1 through 3 in *reverse sequence* until the examinee obtains perfect scores on two consecutive items. The subtest is discontinued after four consecutive failures.

Rationale. The rationale presented for the WISC–III Comprehension subtest also applies to the WAIS–III Comprehension subtest (see Appendix J, page 1088).

Factor analytic findings. The Comprehension subtest is a good measure of g (59 percent of its variance may be attributed to g). This subtest contributes substantially to the Verbal Comprehension factor (Average loading = .81). Specificity is ample or adequate for six age groups (16–17, 18–19, 20–24, 30–34, 70–74, 80–84 years); at seven age groups (25–29, 35–44,

45–54, 55–64, 65–69, 75–79, 85–89 years) it is inadequate.

Reliability and correlational highlights. Comprehension is a reliable subtest (r_{xx} = .84), with reliability coefficients at or above .79 in each of the 13 age groups (range of .79 to .87). It correlates better with Vocabulary (r = .75), Information (r = .70), and Similarities (r = .70) than with any of the other subtests. It has a moderately high correlation with the Full Scale (r = .75), the Verbal Scale (r = .76), and the Performance Scale (r = .62).

Administrative and interpretive considerations. The administrative and interpretive considerations presented for the WISC–III Comprehension subtest also are relevant for the WAIS–III (see Appendix J, pages 1088–1089). Carefully study the Sample Responses section in the *WAIS–III Administration and Scoring Manual* so that you will know which responses require further inquiry, indicated by (Q). The examples indicate that some 0- and 1-point responses should be queried.

Letter–Number Sequencing

The Letter–Number Sequencing subtest, a supplementary subtest, contains seven items, each consisting of three trials. Each trial requires the examinee to order sequentially a series of numbers and letters that are orally presented in a specified random order. All examinees begin with item 1, and testing is discontinued after failure on all three trials of an item. Letter–Number Sequencing is not used in the computation of the IQ when the six standard Verbal Scale subtests are administered. Although Letter–Number Sequencing is a supplementary subtest, administering it may give you useful diagnostic or clinical information, especially when the examinee may have problems with attention. Also, you will need to administer the subtest to be able to compute the Working Memory Index score.

Rationale. To complete the Letter–Number Sequencing subtest successfully, the examinee must (a) simultaneously track letters and numbers, (b) arrange the numbers in ascending order, (c) arrange the letters in alphabetical order following the numbers, and (d) perform both mental operations without forgetting any part of the series. The Letter–Number Sequencing subtest involves attention, short-term memory, and information processing. The *WAIS–III–WMS–III Technical Manual* (The Psychological Corporation, 1997) identifies the construct measured by this task as *working memory*—a dynamic short-term memory storage system of limited capacity, used to hold information that is being processed (Baddley, 1990).

Factor analytic findings. The Letter–Number Sequencing subtest is a fair measure of *g* (42 percent of its variance may be attributed to *g*). This subtest contributes substantially to the Working Memory factor (Average loading = .61). Specificity is either ample or adequate for five age groups (18–19, 30–34, 45–54, 70–74, 85–89 years); at eight age groups (16–17, 20–24, 25–29, 35–44, 55–64, 65–69, 75–79, 80–84 years) it is inadequate.

Reliability and correlational highlights. Letter–Number Sequencing is a reliable subtest (r_{xx} = .82), with reliability coefficients at or above .75 in each of the 13 age groups (range of .75 to .88). It correlates better with Digit Span (r = .57) and Arithmetic (r = .55) than with any of the other subtests. It has a moderately high correlation with the Full Scale (r = .64) and the Verbal Scale (r = .62) and a moderate correlation with the Performance Scale (r = .57).

Administrative and interpretive considerations. Read the numbers and letters clearly, at the rate of one per second. Practice reading speed with a stopwatch. Never repeat any of the numbers or letters on any trial of a series during the subtest proper. Be sure to administer all of the practice items. If an examinee fails a practice item, correct him or her and repeat the instructions as necessary. Even if all the practice items are failed, proceed with the items on the subtest.

Always administer all three trials of each series. Give the examinee credit for each trial that she or he passes. Also give credit to any response that is in correct sequence, regardless of whether the numbers or the letters are said first. Thus, for example, for item 1, trial 1, give credit to the response "L-2." (David Tulsky of The Psychological Corporation supports this procedure, personal communication, May 1998.) Whenever you have any doubt about the examinee's auditory acuity, request an audiological examination. Because this subtest contains no cues (that is, you present only a random series of letters and numbers), hard-of-hearing examinees may be especially prone to failure. On the

Record Form you can record the letters and numbers correctly recalled in each series either by placing a check mark above each letter or digit correctly recalled or by putting a mark designating an incorrect answer on each letter or number missed. A better procedure, however, is to record the exact response given by the examinee in the available space on the Record Form.

A good record can help you evaluate the examinee's performance. For example, an examinee who consistently fails to recall the last item in a letter-number series (for "T-9-A-3," says "3-9-A") is different from an examinee who says an incorrect letter (for "T-9-A-3," says "3-9-A-D"). Failing to recall a letter or number may reflect poor attention-concentration, whereas mistaking T for D may reflect an auditory discrimination problem. Unfortunately, the scoring system does not distinguish among failure patterns. For example, an examinee who places one letter out of sequence in a six-item series obtains the same score as an examinee who misses all six items, even though the second examinee's performance is more inefficient than the first examinee's. Finally, although the examinee who gives the letters first and then the numbers receives credit, he or she is demonstrating poor understanding of the directions or inability to follow the directions.

Picture Completion

The Picture Completion subtest requires the examinee to identify the single most important missing detail in 25 drawings of common objects, animals, or people, such as a chair, cow, and face. The examinee's task is to name or point to the essential missing portion of the incomplete picture within the 20-second time limit. The pictures are shown one at a time, and each item is scored 1 or 0 (pass-fail). Administration always begins with item 6. If the examinee passes both items 6 and 7, give credit for items 1 through 5. If the examinee earns a score of 0 on either item 6 or item 7, administer items 1 through 5 in *reverse order* until the examinee has two consecutive passes. The subtest is discontinued after five consecutive failures.

Rationale. The rationale described for the WISC–III Picture Completion subtest also applies to the WAIS–III Picture Completion subtest (see Appendix J, page 1092).

Factor analytic findings. The Picture Completion subtest is a fair measure of *g* (41 percent of its variance may be attributed to *g*). This subtest contributes moderately to the Perceptual Organization factor (Average loading = .48). Specificity is ample at 12 of the 13 age groups; for one age group (80–84 years) it is inadequate.

Reliability and correlational highlights. Picture Completion is a reliable subtest (r_{xx} = .83), with reliability coefficients at or above .76 in each of the 13 age groups (range of .76 to .88). It correlates better with Block Design (r = .52) and Object Assembly (r = .52) than with any of the other subtests. It has a moderately high correlation with the Full Scale (r = .60) and the Performance Scale (r = .60) and a moderate correlation with the Verbal Scale (r = .53).

Administrative and interpretive considerations. The administrative and interpretive considerations presented for the WISC–III Picture Completion subtest apply to the WAIS–III also (see Appendix J).

Digit Symbol—Coding

The Digit Symbol—Coding subtest is similar to Coding B on the WISC–III. The subtest requires the examinee to copy symbols that are paired with numbers. The sample (or key) consists of nine boxes, each of which contains one of the numbers 1 through 9 and a symbol. Each test box contains a number in the upper portion and an empty space in the lower portion. In the empty space, the examinee must draw the symbol that was paired with the number in the key. There are seven practice boxes, followed by 133 boxes in the subtest proper. Both you and the examinee should use pencils without erasers. It is important that the examinee have a smooth drawing surface. One point is allotted for each correct item. The time limit is 120 seconds; no time-bonus points are awarded.

The Digit Symbol—Coding subtest contains two optional procedures. They are intended to help you determine what skills may be deficient if the examinee performs poorly on the subtest; they are not used to compute IQs. *Digit Symbol—Incidental Learning* is a measure of the examinee's ability to recall (a) the associated number-symbol pairs and (b) the individual symbols, independent of the numbers. This procedure is administered immediately after the Digit Symbol—Coding subtest and is untimed. If you administer Digit Symbol—Incidental Learning, be sure that the examinee completes at least four rows of symbols on the initial subtest. Some examinees may need more than 120 seconds to meet this requirement; symbols completed after the time limit do not count in the Digit Symbol—Coding score.

The second optional procedure is administered at the end of the WAIS–III and is called *Digit Symbol—Copy*. This task, which is in a separate Response Booklet, requires the examinee to draw on the blank below the box the symbol that appears in the box. The nine symbols used in the standard Digit Symbol—Coding subtest are the stimuli to be copied. There are seven practice boxes, followed by 133 test boxes. Both you and the examinee should use pencils without erasers, and the surface for drawing should be smooth. One point is allotted for each correct item. The time limit is 90 seconds.

Rationale. The rationale for the WISC–III Coding B subtest also applies to the WAIS–III Digit Symbol—Coding subtest (see Appendix J, pages 1093–1094). The optional procedures are intended to help you determine the reason for a deficient performance on Digit Symbol—Coding. Let's look at three examples. First, a low score on Digit Symbol—Coding, a low score on Digit Symbol—Incidental Learning, and an average score on Digit Symbol—Copy suggest that the examinee may have performed poorly on Digit Symbol—Coding because he or she did not remember the stimuli. Second, a low score on Digit Symbol—Coding, a low score on Digit Symbol—Copy, and an average score on Digit Symbol—Incidental Learning suggest that the low score on Digit Symbol—Coding may reflect impaired graphomotor speed. Finally, a low score on Digit Symbol—Coding, a low score on Digit Symbol—Incidental Learning, and a low score on Digit Symbol—Copy suggest that the low score on Digit Symbol—Coding may reflect impaired memory as well as impaired graphomotor speed. Of course, other interpretations exist, such as poor concentration, inattention, or limited motivation.

Factor analytic findings. Digit Symbol—Coding is a fair measure of g (35 percent of its variance may be attributed to g). This subtest contributes substantially to the Processing Speed factor (Average loading = .73). Specificity is ample for all age groups.

Reliability and correlational highlights. Digit Symbol—Coding is a reliable subtest (r_{xx} = .84), with reliability coefficients at or above .81 in each of the 13 age groups (range of .81 to .87). It correlates better with Symbol Search (r = .65) than with any of the other subtests. It has a moderate correlation with the Full Scale (r = .53) and the Performance Scale (r = .50) and a moderately low correlation with the Verbal Scale (r = .49).

Administrative and interpretive considerations. The administrative and interpretive considerations for the WISC–III Coding B subtest generally apply to the WAIS–III Digit Symbol—Coding subtest (see Appendix J, pages 1094–1095). Because a left-handed examinee would occasionally cover the sample immediately above the line of writing, the space between the key and the stimulus items has been increased. A separate Response Booklet is used for the optional procedures of Digit Symbol—Incidental Learning and Digit Symbol—Copy. Be sure to put the examinee's name, the date, and your name at the top of the Response Booklet. Sometimes an examinee may stop after he or she completes the first row. In such cases, give the Response Booklet back to the examinee, point to the second row, and say "Please complete the second row as well." (David Tulsky of The Psychological Corporation advised that the above directions be used in such instances; personal communication, May 1998.)

Note that there is an error in the Response Booklet for Digit Symbol—Copy (page 7). For the first item in the second row (#14), the Response Booklet shows a three-sided U-shaped figure open to the left. However, the Digit Symbol Scoring Template for this item shows a three-sided U-shaped figure open at the top. Therefore, examinees will receive no credit for an accurate copy of the figure. We recommend that for this item you give credit to a drawing of a three-sided U-shaped figure open to the left and disregard what is shown on the Scoring Template.

Block Design

The Block Design subtest contains 14 items. The examinee is shown a two-dimensional, red-and-white picture of abstract design and then must assemble a design that is identical to the picture, using three-dimensional red and white plastic blocks. All blocks contain the identical surfaces—namely, two red surfaces, two white surfaces, and two red-and-white surfaces. For items 1 through 5, the examinee is shown a model that you construct, and she or he is asked to reproduce the model. All examinees begin with item 5. If an examinee obtains 2 points on both items 5 and 6, she or he receives full credit for items 1 through 4. If an examinee scores 0 or 1 on either item 5 or item 6, administer items 1 through 4 in *reverse order* until the examinee earns two consecutive perfect scores.

The patterns are arranged in order of increasing difficulty. Two blocks are used for items 1 and 2, four blocks are needed to reproduce items 3 through 9, and nine blocks are required for items 10 through 14. All items are timed. The time limits are 30 seconds for items 1 through 4, 60 seconds for items 5 through 9, and 120 seconds for items 10 through 14. On items 1 through 6, the examinee is given 2 points for successful completion on the first trial and 1 point for successful completion on the second trial. On items 7 through 14, the examinee receives 4 points for a correct completion and is awarded up to 3 additional time-bonus points for quick execution. The subtest is discontinued after three consecutive failures.

Rationale. The rationale presented for the WISC–III Block Design subtest also applies to the WAIS–III Block Design (see Appendix J, page 1097).

Factor analytic findings. The Block Design subtest is tied with Matrix Reasoning as the best measure of g among the Performance Scale subtests (52 percent of its variance may be attributed to g). This subtest contributes substantially to the Perceptual Organization factor (Average loading = .70). Specificity is either ample or adequate for all age groups.

Reliability and correlational highlights. Block Design is a reliable subtest (r_{xx} = .86), with reliability coefficients at or above .76 in each of the

13 age groups (range of .76 to .90). It correlates better with Object Assembly (r = .61) and Matrix Reasoning (r = .60) than with any of the other subtests. It has a moderately high correlation with the Full Scale (r = .66) and the Performance Scale (r = .66) and a moderate correlation with the Verbal Scale (r = .59).

Administrative and interpretive considerations. The administrative and interpretive considerations described for the WISC–III Block Design subtest generally apply to the WAIS–III (see Appendix J, page 1098). Timing and bonus points differ on the two subtests, however.

Following are some additional suggestions for evaluating an examinee's performance on the Block Design subtest. If time permits, after the examinee has completed the entire test, you can go back to the subtest and show the examinee some of his or her incorrect reproductions, one at a time. Ask the examinee if the reproduction is the same as or different from the original design. If the examinee recognizes that his or her design is incorrect and can tell you the specific errors (e.g., "A red-and-white block goes here, not a white block"), the examinee may have a visual-motor execution problem. Recognize that this testing-of-limits procedure and similar procedures used with other subtests may invalidate the WAIS–III for future assessments—assessments needed to monitor treatment or rehabilitation programs, for example.

You also can use other constructional tasks (e.g., the Bender-Gestalt or the Greek Cross item from the Reitan-Indiana Aphasia Screening Test; see Chapters 14 and 22, respectively) to investigate a hypothesis of impaired visuospatial manipulation and motor output. For example, discovering that the examinee has difficulty reproducing the Bender-Gestalt designs, recognizes her or his errors, but can't improve the designs on repeated attempts would be consistent with an hypothesis of impaired visual-motor output.

Matrix Reasoning

The Matrix Reasoning subtest is composed of 26 nonverbal reasoning tasks that involve pattern completion, analogy, classification, or serial reasoning. The items consist of individually presented colored matrixes, each of which is missing a part. The examinee is directed to look at all aspects of each matrix carefully and select the missing part from an array of five choices at the bottom of the page. Each examinee begins with three sample items (A, B, and C), which are intended to help him or her understand the instructions on the subtest, and then is given item 4. If the examinee answers items 4 and 5 correctly, give credit for items 1, 2, and 3. If the examinee fails either item 4 or item 5, administer items 1, 2, and 3 in *reverse sequence* until the examinee passes two consecutive items. The subtest is untimed, and it is discontinued after either (a) four consecutive failures or (b) four failures in five consecutive items.

Rationale. The Matrix Reasoning subtest involves perceptual reasoning ability. Analogic reasoning, attention to detail, and concentration are required for successful performance. Additionally, spatial ability may be involved for some examinees. Experience with part-whole relationships may be helpful, as may a willingness to respond when uncertain.

Factor analytic findings. The Matrix Reasoning subtest is tied with Block Design as the second best measure of g in the Performance Scale (52 percent of its variance may be attributed to g). This subtest contributes moderately to the Perceptual Organization factor (Average loading = .49) and to a limited extent to the Working Memory factor (Average loading = .33).

Reliability and correlational highlights. Matrix Reasoning is a reliable subtest (r_{xx} = .90), with reliability coefficients at or above .84 in each of the 13 age groups (range of .84 to .94). It correlates better with Block Design (r = .60) and Arithmetic (r = .58) than with any of the other subtests. It has a moderately high correlation with the Full Scale (r = .69), the Performance Scale (r = .65), and the Verbal Scale (r = .64).

Administrative and interpretive considerations. Matrix Reasoning is relatively easy to administer. Simply leave the stimulus booklet flat on the table and turn the cards over one at a time to show each item. The examinee may respond orally or by pointing. You can administer the teaching items (A, B, and C) more than once if needed. You can also give the examinee as much help as she or he needs in order for her or him to understand how the subtest works. After you complete the teaching items, proceed to item 4 even if the examinee fails items A, B, and C.

Observe the examinee carefully for signs of impulsivity (i.e., examinee responds without examining the stimulus) as well as for signs of visual difficulties. Also, be alert to the possibility of a response set on the part of the examinee. A response set is indicated if the examinee points to the same numbered choice for each item. After you administer the subtest, you can inquire about the examinee's approach to the task in order to gain insight into her or his problem-solving strategies.

Picture Arrangement

The Picture Arrangement subtest requires the examinee to arrange a series of pictures in a logical sequence. Each of the 11 series of pictures is presented in a specified disarranged order, and the examinee is asked to rearrange the pictures in the "right" order to tell a story. One set of cards is presented at a time. Little motor action is required, as the pictures simply must be shifted to make a meaningful story. All examinees begin with item 1. The first item has two trials and is scored 2, 1, or 0. Items 2 through 4 and items 10 and 11 are scored either 0 or 2; items 5 through 9 are scored 0, 1, or 2. On items 5 through 9, 1 point is given for an acceptable variation of the correct arrangement. Time limits are 30 seconds for each trial of item 1, 45 seconds for item 2, 60 seconds for items 3 and 4, 90 seconds for items 5 and 6, and 120 seconds for items 7 through 11.

Rationale. The rationale presented for the WISC–III Picture Arrangement subtest also applies to the WAIS–III Picture Arrangement subtest (see Appendix J, page 1095).

Factor analytic findings. The Picture Arrangement subtest is a fair measure of g (44 percent of its variance may be attributed to g). This subtest contributes to a limited extent to the Perceptual Organization factor (Average loading = .35) and to the Verbal Comprehension factor (Average loading = .31). Specificity is either ample or adequate for six age groups (16–17, 25–29, 35–44, 65–69, 70–74, 85–89 years); at seven age groups (18–19, 20–24, 30–34, 45–54, 55–64, 75–79, 80–84 years) it is inadequate.

Reliability and correlational highlights. Picture Arrangement is relatively reliable (r_{xx} = .74), with reliability coefficients at or above .66 in each of the 13 age groups (range of .66 to .81).

It correlates better with Information (r = .54) and Vocabulary (r = .53) than with any of the other subtests. It has a moderately high correlation with the Full Scale (r = .63) and the Performance Scale (r = .60) and a moderate correlation with the Verbal Scale (r = .59).

Administrative and interpretive considerations. The administrative and interpretive considerations presented for the WISC–III Picture Arrangement subtest generally apply to the WAIS–III (see Appendix J, pages 1096–1097). However, the bonus points awarded on the WISC–III Picture Arrangement subtest for speed are not awarded on the WAIS–III Picture Arrangement subtest.

Symbol Search

The Symbol Search subtest, a supplementary subtest, requires the examinee to look at two symbols and decide whether either symbol is present in an array of five symbols. The subtest contains 60 items and has a time limit of 120 seconds. The score is the total number of correct items minus the number of incorrect items. There are no time-bonus credits.

Rationale. The rationale presented for the WISC–III Symbol Search subtest also applies to the WAIS–III Symbol Search subtest (see Appendix J, pages 1100–1101).

Factor analytic findings. The Symbol Search subtest is a fair measure of g (49 percent of its variance may be attributed to g). This subtest contributes substantially to the Processing Speed factor (Average loading = .70). Specificity is either ample or adequate for three age groups (30–34, 35–44, 45–54 years); at 10 age groups (16–17, 18–19, 20–24, 25–29, 55–64, 65–69, 70–74, 75–79, 80–84, 85–89 years) it is inadequate.

Reliability and correlational highlights. Symbol Search is a relatively reliable subtest (r_{xx} = .77), with reliability coefficients at or above .74 in each of the 13 age groups (range of .74 to .82). It correlates better with Digit Symbol—Coding (r = .65) than with any of the other subtests. It has a moderately high correlation with the Full Scale (r = .66) and the Performance Scale (r = .69) and a moderate correlation with the Verbal Scale (r = .57).

Administrative and interpretive considerations. The administrative and interpretive considerations presented for the WISC–III Symbol Search subtest generally apply to the WAIS–III (see Appendix J, pages 1101–1102). However, unlike the WISC–III Symbol Search, the WAIS–III Symbol Search subtest has only one form, and each item has two, rather than one, target symbols.

Object Assembly

The Object Assembly subtest, which is an optional subtest, requires the examinee to put jigsaw pieces together to form common objects: a manikin (6 pieces), a profile of a face (7 pieces), an elephant (6 pieces), a house (9 pieces), and a butterfly (7 pieces). The items are administered one at a time, with the pieces presented in a specified disarranged pattern. Examinees are administered all five items.

All items are timed. The first two items have a time limit of 120 seconds each; and the last three items, 180 seconds each. The manikin has a maximum score of 8; the face, 12; the elephant, 11; the house, 10; and the butterfly, 11. Up to three bonus points are awarded on each item for quick execution. Points also are awarded for partially correct performances.

Rationale. The rationale presented for the WISC–III Object Assembly subtest also applies to the WAIS–III Object Assembly subtest (see Appendix J, page 1099).

Factor analytic findings. The Object Assembly subtest is a fair measure of g (38 percent of its variance may be attributed to g). This subtest contributes substantially to the Perceptual Organization factor (Average loading = .74). Specificity is adequate for one age group (45–54 years); at the other 12 age groups it is inadequate.

Reliability and correlational highlights. Object Assembly is the least reliable of the WAIS–III subtests (r_{xx} = .70), with reliability coefficients at or above .50 in each of the 13 age groups (range of .50 to .75). It correlates better with Block Design (r = .61) than with any of the other subtests. It has a moderate correlation with the Full Scale (r = .59), a moderately high correlation with the Performance Scale (r = .64), and a moderate correlation with the Verbal Scale (r = .50).

Administrative and interpretive considerations. The administrative and interpretive considerations described for the WISC–III Object Assembly subtest generally apply to the WAIS–III (see Appendix J, pages 1099–1100).

Question: Where is the English Channel?
Answer: I don't know. My TV doesn't get that channel.

INTERPRETING THE WAIS–III

Almost all of the material in Appendix K on interpreting the WISC–III pertains to the WAIS–III. For example, the successive level approach to test interpretation, profile analysis, Verbal-Performance Scale comparisons, factor score (or Index score) comparisons, and subtest comparisons are similar for both tests. The estimated percentile ranks for subtest scaled scores are shown in Table C-41 in Appendix C (page 855). This table also shows suggested qualitative descriptions associated with scaled scores. Table BC-2 on the inside back cover shows the classifications associated with WAIS–III IQs. (Note, however, that the WAIS–III uses "Extremely Low" in place of "Mentally Retarded" for IQs of 69 and below.) In Appendix C, Table C-13 (page 824) summarizes the functions associated with 12 of the 14 subtests (substitute Digit Symbol—Coding for Coding); the two subtests not covered in the table are Matrix Reasoning and Symbol Search. Table C-42 (page 856) presents information about the three scales and two of the four Index scores (Working Memory and Processing Speed are not covered in the table), and Table C-43 (page 858) gives suggested remediation activities for combinations of Wechsler subtests.

Profile Analysis

As noted above, approaches to profile analysis are basically the same on the WAIS–III as on the WISC–III (see Appendix K, pages 1106–1108). The main difference is that you must use the tables in Appendix O of this text for the WAIS–III. The approach to profile analysis that follows is a combined one; differences between IQs and scaled scores are examined based on both statistical significance and base rates of such differences that occur in the standardization sample.

1. *Comparing Verbal and Performance IQs*. Table O-2 in Appendix O provides critical values for comparing the Verbal and Performance IQs for 16- to 17-year-olds, for 18- to 19-year-olds, and for the average of the standardization sample. For examinees 16 to 17 years old and for examinees 18 to 19 years old, a difference of **10** points is required at the .05 level and **13** points at the .01 level. The critical values are **9** at the .05 level and **12** at the .01 level for the average of the standardization group. The values in Table O-2 range from 7 to 10 at the .05 level and from 10 to 13 at the .01 level. Thus, an average critical value based on the entire standardization sample would be misleading in some cases (compare Table O-2 with Table B.1 on page 205 of the *WAIS–III Administration and Scoring Manual*). Therefore, use the values for a specific age group to evaluate differences between an examinee's Verbal and Performance IQs. Table O-4 in Appendix O shows the probabilities associated with various differences between the WAIS–III Verbal and Performance Scale IQs.

Table B.2 (pp. 206–207) in the *WAIS–III Administration and Scoring Manual* shows the cumulative percentages in the standardization sample that obtained various Verbal-Performance IQ differences in both directions. The mean Verbal-Performance difference in both directions was 8.6, and the median difference in both directions was 7.0. Approximately 20 percent of the sample had a Verbal-Performance difference in one or the other direction of 14 points or higher, and approximately 81 percent of the sample had a Verbal-Performance difference in one or the other direction of 3 points or higher.

The cumulative percentages shown in Table B.2 of the *WAIS–III Administration and Scoring Manual* are absolute values (i.e., they represent bi-directional differences, combining both Verbal > Performance and Performance > Verbal values). In the first printing of the manual, there is no statement that the cumulative frequencies in Table B.2 are absolute values. Unfortunately, Table B.2 does not provide the frequencies with which differences between the Verbal and Performance IQs occurred in the standardization sample in either direction alone. Without this information, it is difficult to determine the actual occurrence in the standardization sample of each kind of difference between the Verbal and Performance IQs. An examinee can have a Verbal-Performance discrepancy in one direction only. *Therefore, we suggest that you divide all of the frequencies in Table B.2 by 2 when you complete the last column of the Discrepancy Analysis Page, which is called "Frequency of difference in standardization sample," to obtain the base rate.* (David Tulsky of The Psychological Corporation supports this procedure; personal communications, April 1998 and May 1998. Dr. Tulsky also said that in the next printing of the manual the following footnote will be added: "The differences between IQ and Index Scores are non-directional; for example, a difference of 26 points refers to PIQ minus VIQ and to VIQ minus PIQ and it was obtained by 2 percent of the sample. If the values are divided by two, they will approximate the differences between IQ and Index Scores had they been directional.") Thus, for example, a difference of 10 points between a Verbal IQ of 120 and a Performance IQ of 110 likely occurred in approximately 18.6 percent of the standardization sample, not the 37.2 percent shown in Table B.2. We need research to learn about the frequency of Verbal IQs > Performance IQs and Performance IQs > Verbal IQs in every age group in the standardization sample. Until such research is available, dividing the frequencies by 2 is probably the best way to estimate the frequencies with which differences between IQs occurred in one direction in the standardization sample.

Our recommended procedure differs from the one stated in the *WAIS–III Administration and Scoring Manual*. Page 61 of the manual says "Using Table B.2, find the difference obtained by the examinee in the Amount of Discrepancy column. Then, read across the row to the column corresponding to the relevant discrepancy score (e.g., VIQ–PIQ). Record that value in the appropriate space on the Discrepancy Analysis Page of the Record Form." As noted above, the values in Table B.2 are absolute values. Therefore, they should not be used without modification to determine the frequency with which any one examinee's Verbal-Performance discrepancy occurred in the standardization sample.

Tables D.1 to D.5 (pp. 300–309) in the *WAIS–III—WMS–III Technical Manual* present the frequency distributions of Verbal-Performance IQ differences in both directions at five ability levels; these again are absolute values. These tables indicate that the magnitude of differences in both directions increases as IQ level increases. The mean differences as a function of IQ level were as follows: IQ ≤ 79: 6.1; IQ 80–89: 6.0; IQ 90–109: 8.6; IQ 110–119: 9.6; IQ ≥ 120: 10.3. When we look at specific differences, we find, for example, that a 10-point difference in one or the other direction occurred in 20.6 percent of individuals with a Full Scale IQ less than or equal to 79, whereas 48.1 percent of individuals with a Full Scale IQ greater than or equal to 120 had a 10-point difference in one or the other direction. Thus, individuals with lower IQs have a smaller average Verbal-Performance difference than those with higher IQs.

We recommend that you use the values for the examinee's specific ability range in Tables D.1 to D.5 of the *WAIS–III—WMS–III Technical Manual* to establish the base rate for differences between the Verbal and Performance IQs. *These values also must be divided by 2 to get an estimate of the base rate of Verbal-Performance differences for one direction only.*

2. *Comparing each Verbal subtest scaled score with the mean Verbal scaled score.* Table O-3 in Appendix O provides critical values for comparing each of the Verbal subtests with the mean of the standard six subtests or the mean of the standard six Verbal subtests plus Letter–Number Sequencing. The critical values range from 2.02 to 2.83 at the .05 level and from 2.41 to 3.36 at the .01 level when the standard six Verbal subtests are administered. The critical values range from 2.09 to 3.15 at the .05 level and from 2.48 to 3.72 at the .01 level when seven subtests are considered. Also provided are the critical values for comparing each Verbal subtest with the mean of six subtests when Letter–Number Sequencing is substituted for Digit Span.

Table B.3 (pp. 208–209) in the *WAIS–III Administration and Scoring Manual* gives the cumulative frequencies with which various differences occurred in the standardization sample between an examinee's scaled score on each subtest and his or her average WAIS–III Verbal scaled score. The table shows, for example, that a difference of 2.83 points between the scaled score on Vocabulary and the Verbal Scale average, composed of scores on the six standard subtests, was obtained by 5 percent of the standardization sample. Use this table only for differences that have first been shown to be reliable (that is, see the significance level columns in Table B.3 in the *WAIS–III Administration and Scoring Manual* or Table O-3 in Appendix O). Differences of 2.83 to 4.00 points between each subtest scaled score and the average Verbal Scale score were obtained by 5 percent of the standardization sample.

3. *Comparing each Performance subtest scaled score with the mean Performance scaled score.* Table O-3 in Appendix O provides critical values for comparing each of the Performance subtests with the mean of the standard five subtests, the mean of the standard five Performance subtests plus Symbol Search, the mean of the standard five subtests plus Object Assembly, or the mean of the standard five subtests plus both Symbol Search and Object Assembly. The critical values range from 2.40 to 3.37 at the .05 level and from 2.88 to 4.04 at the .01 level when the five standard Performance subtests are administered. The critical values range from 2.50 to 3.57 at the .05 level and from 2.97 to 4.24 at the .01 level when the five standard subtests plus Symbol Search are considered. The critical values range from 2.59 to 4.01 at the .05 level and from 3.07 to 4.75 at the .01 level when all seven Performance subtests are given. Table O-3 also provides the critical values for comparing each Performance subtest with the mean of six subtests when Symbol Search is substituted for Object Assembly.

Table B.3 (pp. 208–209) in the *WAIS–III Administration and Scoring Manual* gives the cumulative frequencies with which various differences occurred in the standardization sample between an examinee's scaled score on each subtest and his or her average WAIS–III Performance scaled score. The table shows, for example, that a difference of 3.8 points (or higher) between the scaled score on Picture Completion and the Performance Scale average, composed of scores on the five standard subtests, was obtained by 5 percent of the standardization sample. Use this table only for differences that have first been shown to be reliable (that is, see the significance level columns in Table B.3 in the *WAIS–III Administration and Scoring Manual* or Table O-3 in Appendix O). Differences of 3.6 to 4.4 between each subtest scaled score and the average Performance Scale score were obtained by 5 percent of the standardization sample.

4. *Comparing each subtest scaled score with the mean of (a) the standard 11 subtests, (b) the standard 11 subtests plus Letter–Number Sequencing, (c) the standard 11 subtests plus Letter–Number Sequencing and Symbol Search, and (d) all 14 subtests.* Table O-3 in Appendix O provides critical values for comparing subtest scaled scores with the mean of the standard 11 subtests. They range from 2.24 to 4.05 at the .05 level and from 2.62 to 4.73 at the .01 level. When Letter–Number Sequencing is added, critical values range from 2.27 to 4.12 at the .05 level and from 2.64 to 4.79 at the .01 level. When both Letter–Number Sequencing and Symbol Search are added, critical values range from 2.30 to 4.17 at the .05 level and from 2.67 to 4.85 at the .01 level. If all 14 subtests are administered, the critical values range from 2.33 to 4.58 at the .05 level and from 2.69 to 5.29 at the .01 level.

Table B.3 (pp. 208–209) in the *WAIS–III Administration and Scoring Manual* gives the cumulative frequencies with which various differences occurred in the standardization sample between an examinee's scaled score on each subtest and her or his average WAIS–III scaled score based on the 11 standard subtests and on the 11 Index score subtests. The table shows, for example, that a difference of 3.36 points (or higher) between the scaled score on Vocabulary and the mean scaled score, composed of scores on the 11 standard subtests, was obtained by 5 percent of the standardization sample. Use this table only for differences that have first been shown to be reliable (that is, see the significance level columns in Table B.3 in the *WAIS–III Administration and Scoring Manual* or Table O-3 in Appendix O). Differences of 3.36 to 4.82 points between each subtest scaled score and the mean scaled score were obtained by 5 percent of the standardization sample.

5. *Comparing each subtest scaled score with the mean of (a) the 11 standard subtests, but with Letter–Number Sequencing substituted for Digit Span, and (b) the standard 11 subtests, but with Symbol Search in place of Digit Symbol—Coding.* Table O-3 in Appendix O provides critical values for comparing subtest scaled scores with the mean of the 11 subtests when Letter–Number Sequencing is substituted for Digit Span. They range from 2.26 to 4.05 at the .05 level and from 2.64 to 4.74 at the .01 level. When Symbol Search is substituted for Digit Symbol—Coding, critical values range

from 2.25 to 4.05 at the .05 level and from 2.63 to 4.73 at the .01 level.

6. *Comparing pairs of individual subtest scaled scores.* Table O-2 in Appendix O provides critical values for comparing sets of subtest scaled scores. The values range between 3 and 5 scaled-score points at the .05 level and between 4 and 6 scaled-score points at the .01 level. The values in Table O-2 for subtest comparisons are overly liberal (that is, they lead to significant differences that may not actually be true differences) when more than one comparison is made. They are most accurate when a priori planned comparisons are made, such as Comprehension versus Picture Arrangement or Digit Span versus Arithmetic. (See Chapter 8 for additional information that can guide interpretations of subtest comparisons.)

Before making *multiple comparisons*, determine the difference between the highest and lowest subtest scores. If this difference is 6 scaled-score points or more, a significant difference at the .05 level is indicated. You can then interpret differences of 6 scaled-score points or more between subtests. If the difference between the highest and lowest subtest scaled scores is less than 6 scaled-score points, do not make multiple comparisons between individual subtest scores. (The Note to Table H-2 on page 1015 in Appendix H shows the formula used to compute the significant difference. The formula considers the average standard error of measurement for each of the 14 subtests and the studentized range statistic.)

7. *Comparing Verbal Comprehension, Perceptual Organization, Working Memory, and Processing Speed Index scores.* Table O-2 in Appendix O presents the differences between sets of Verbal Comprehension, Perceptual Organization, Working Memory, and Processing Speed Index scores (in the form of Deviation IQs) needed to reach the .05 and .01 significance levels for 16- to 17-year-olds, for 18- to 19-year-olds, and for the average of the standardization sample. Table O-5 in Appendix O shows probabilities associated with various differences between WAIS–III Index scores.

Table B.2 (pp. 206–207) in the *WAIS–III Administration and Scoring Manual* also shows the cumulative percentages in the standardization group that obtained various Index score differences in both directions. As with the Verbal-Performance differences, the cumulative percentages shown in Table B.2 are absolute values (i.e., they represent bi-directional differences). *Therefore, we again suggest that in evaluating the differences between Index scores, you divide all of the frequencies in Table B.2 by 2 when you complete the last column of the Discrepancy Analysis Page, which is called "Frequency of difference in standardization sample," to obtain the base rate Index score differences that occurred in one direction only.*

Tables D.1 to D.5 (pp. 300–309) in the *WAIS–III—WMS–III Technical Manual* present the frequency distributions of pairs of Index score differences in both directions at five ability levels; these again are absolute values. As with the Verbal and Performance IQs, the differences between pairs of Index scores vary in relationship to Full Scale IQ as well as to the type of comparison under consideration. For example, the mean difference between Working Memory and Processing Speed was 10.3 in either direction for individuals with a Full Scale IQ less than or equal to 79, whereas the mean difference was 13.7 in either direction for individuals with a Full Scale IQ greater than or equal to 120; and the mean difference between Perceptual Organization and Processing Speed was 7.5 in either direction for individuals with a Full Scale IQ less than or equal to 79, whereas the mean difference was 12.2 in either direction for individuals with a Full Scale IQ greater than or equal to 120. We recommend that you use the values for the examinee's specific ability range in Tables D.1 to D.5 of the *WAIS–III—WMS–III Technical Manual* to establish the base rate for differences between the Index scores. *These values also must be divided by 2 to get an estimate of differences between the Index scores for one direction only.*

8. *Comparing subtest scaled scores in each Index with their respective Index mean.* Table O-3 in Appendix O provides the critical values for comparing WAIS–III subtest scaled scores in the total sample with their respective Index mean. Critical values for the Verbal Comprehension Index range from 1.70 to 2.03 at the .05 level and from 2.09 to 2.48 at the .01 level. For the Perceptual Organization Index, they range from 2.05 to 2.32 at the .05 level and from 2.51 to 2.85 at the .01 level. For the Working Memory Index, they range from 2.00 to 2.36 at the .05 level and from 2.46 to 2.89 at the .01 level. For the Processing Speed Index, they are 2.08 at the .05 level and 2.61 at the .01 level.

9. *Comparing the examinee's subtest scaled-score range to the range found in the standardization sample.* The subtest scaled-score range provides information about the variability (or scatter) in an examinee's WAIS–III profile. The scaled-score range indicates the distance between the two most extreme scaled scores. It is obtained by subtracting the lowest scaled score from the highest scaled score. For example, in a profile where the highest scaled score is 15 and the lowest scaled score is 3, the range is 12, since 15 − 3 = 12.

In the standardization sample, the median scaled-score range was 7 points for the 11 standard subtests on the Full Scale, 5 points for the six standard subtests on Verbal Scale, and 5 points for the five standard subtests on the Performance Scale (see Table B.5, p. 211, *WAIS–III Administration and Scoring Manual*). The scaled-score range is based on only two scores and therefore fails to take into account the variability among all 11 (or 12, 13, or 14) subtest scores. However, the range index is still useful because it provides base rate information about what occurred in the standardization sample. It also is a relatively simple measure of variability that can be compared with more complex indices of variability, such as the standard deviation of the 11 subtests and the number of subtests on which scaled scores deviate significantly from the overall mean scaled score. Research on the WAIS–R standardization sample indicated that the range is as useful a measure of variability as is the standard deviation or the number of tests that differ significantly from the mean (Matarazzo, Daniel, Prifitera, & Herman, 1988). However, we need research to determine whether this finding also applies to the WAIS–III.

Statistically Reliable vs. Empirically Observed IQ Differences

We have seen that there are two types of complementary measures that can assist in profile analysis—statistically reliable differences and empirically observed base rates. Table O-2 in Appendix O presents the differences required between Verbal and Performance IQs and between Index scores for statistical significance. Table B.2 on pages 207 and 208 of the *WAIS–III Administration and Scoring Manual* gives the actual (i.e., empirically observed) base rates of the frequencies of differences between the IQs and between the Index scores found in the standardization sample. One table represents statistical significance (Table O-2), and the other is about frequency of occurrence (Table B.2). Whether an occurrence is unusual or rare depends on how one defines "unusual." A difference that occurs in 15 percent or 20 percent of the population may be considered unusual by some, whereas others may consider a difference unusual only if it occurs in 5 percent or 10 percent of the population. We believe that all significant differences, regardless of whether they are unusual or rare, deserve consideration in evaluating an examinee's profile of abilities. However, we also believe that we can be more confident about the hypotheses we form when the difference *also* is unusual or rare. We suggest that, in order to be considered unusual or rare, the difference should occur in 15 percent or less (in one direction) of the standardization sample.

Let's look at two examples. First, an examinee has a Verbal-Performance IQ difference of 9 points, which is significant at the .05 level. This means that the Verbal-Performance IQ difference is reliable and not the result of measurement error (i.e., chance). Differences that are greater than chance may reflect differential functioning in the abilities measured by the Verbal and Performance Scales and Index scores. From Table B.2 we find that a difference of 9 points or more in one direction between the Verbal and Performance IQs occurred in approximately 21.3 percent (42.7 percent in Table B.2 divided by 2) of the standardization sample. This 9-point difference, therefore, is statistically significant but not necessarily unusual or rare. It is an empirical question whether the 9-point difference is clinically meaningful.

Second, an examinee obtains a Verbal-Performance IQ difference of 26 points, which is significant at the .01 level. From Table B.2 we find that a difference of 26 points or more in *one* direction between the Verbal and Performance IQs occurred in approximately 1 percent (2.0 percent in Table B.2 divided by 2) of the standardization sample. This 26-point difference, therefore, is not only statistically significant but also unusual or rare.

Clinical acumen, the examinee's medical history, behavioral observations, and the results of other tests that the examinee has taken will help you interpret differences between Verbal and Performance IQs and differences between Index scores. Recognize that several vari-

ables—such as the examinee's ethnicity, linguistic background, and educational level—may influence the magnitude and direction of the Verbal IQ–Performance IQ relationship. For example, examinees with graduate level education may have significantly higher Verbal than Performance IQs, and examinees with non-English linguistic backgrounds and those from some ethnic minority groups (e.g., Native Americans) may have lower Verbal than Performance IQs (Kaufman, 1990). Therefore, differences between the Verbal and Performance IQs of examinees from non-English linguistic backgrounds are probably related to their language background and should be interpreted accordingly.

Age and WAIS–III Subtest Performance

The age norms on the WAIS–III allow us to determine how scaled-score points are awarded to individuals in each age group as a function of raw-score points (Ryan, Lopez, & Sattler, 1998). Table N-18 was constructed in the following way: First, for each age group in the reference group (ages 20–34 years), we located the raw score associated with the scaled score of 10. Then, for each raw score obtained from the reference group, we located the scaled score associated with that raw score in each age group. This procedure allowed us to compare all of the age groups on every subtest.

Table N-18 indicates that there were few differences between older and younger people in verbal ability, but large differences in nonverbal ability. For example, individuals in the 85–89-year age group (and individuals in other older age groups as well) show little, if any, difference from the reference group (ages 20–34 years) on Information, Vocabulary, and Comprehension (0 or 1 scaled-score points); slight differences on Arithmetic, Similarities, and Digit Span (2 or 3 scaled-score points); a moderate difference on Letter–Number Sequencing (5 scaled-score points); and large differences on all of the Performance Scale subtests (6 to 9 scaled-score points). Within the Performance Scale, measurable differences in ability begin with the 45–54-year age group. Subtests that assess speed of information processing show the greatest difference as one moves from the younger to the older groups. For example, in the reference group (20–34 years), a raw score of 33 on Symbol Search

Table N-18
Additional Scaled-Score Points by Age Group Awarded to WAIS–III Subtests When the Reference Group (Ages 20–34 Years) Receives a Scaled Score of 10

Subtest	16–17	18–19	20–24	25–29	30–34	35–44	45–54	55–64	65–69	70–74	75–79	80–84	85–89
Vocabulary	1	0	0	0	−1	−1	−2	−1	−1	−1	−1	1	1
Similarities	0	0	0	0	−1	−1	−1	0	1	1	1	2	3
Arithmetic	0	0	0	0	−1	−1	−1	−1	0	0	0	1	2
Digit Span	0	0	0	0	0	0	0	1	1	1	2	2	3
Information	0	0	0	0	−1	−1	−2	−1	−1	−1	−1	0	0
Comprehension	1	0	0	0	−1	−1	−2	−1	−1	−1	0	1	1
Letter–Number Seq.	0	0	0	0	0	0	1	2	2	3	4	4	5
Picture Completion	0	0	0	0	0	0	0	1	1	2	3	4	6
Digit Symbol—Coding	0	−1	−1	0	0	0	1	3	4	5	6	7	8
Block Design	0	0	0	0	0	0	1	2	3	4	5	5	6
Matrix Reasoning	−1	0	0	0	0	0	1	2	3	4	5	5	6
Picture Arrangement	0	0	0	0	0	0	1	2	3	4	5	6	6
Symbol Search	0	−1	0	0	0	0	1	2	3	5	6	8	9
Object Assembly	0	0	0	0	0	0	1	2	3	4	6	6	7

Note. Negative values indicate performance that exceeds that of the reference group of persons 20 to 34 years old.

The results in this table indicate that raw scores yielding a scaled score of 10 in the WAIS–III reference group (ages 20–34 years) yield, in most cases, the same or higher scaled scores in the eight age groups over 34 years. The greatest change is at ages 75–89 years. For example, in the reference group a raw score of 76 on Digit Symbol—Coding yields a scaled score of 10, but at ages 85–89 years this same raw score yields a scaled score of 18. The 8 additional scaled-score points awarded at ages 85–89 years change the percentile rank for a raw score of 76 from 50 to 99. Symbol Search exhibits the most change of any WAIS–III subtest, showing a steady increment in scaled-score points from age 45 to age 89.

The greatest changes are consistently shown on the Performance Scale subtests. On the Verbal Scale subtests, the increment in scaled-score points is never greater than 5 points, with most changes being either plus or minus 1 or 2 points. Information, Comprehension, and Vocabulary show the least amount of change with advancing age. The one exception on the Verbal Scale subtests is Letter–Number Sequencing. For this subtest, for a performance that is average in the reference group, 5 additional points are awarded at ages 85–89 years and 4 additional points at ages 75–84 years.

The positive values in this table actually reflect less proficient ability. This is more graphically revealed when the raw-score points needed at the various age groups to obtain an average scaled score are examined. For example, as we have seen, on Digit Symbol—Coding a raw score of 76 yields a scaled score of 10 for the reference group. At ages 85 to 89 years, however, a raw score of only 33 is required to obtain a scaled score of 10. Thus, individuals in the oldest age group need 43 fewer raw-score points than do those in the reference group to obtain average status in their age group.

yields a scaled score of 10. However, at ages 85–89 years, the same raw score yields a scaled score of 19. Similarly, in the reference group, a raw score of 76 on Digit Symbol—Coding yields a scaled score of 10. However, at ages 85–89 years, the same raw score yields a scaled score of 18. The 9 and 8 additional scaled-score points awarded at ages 85–89 years change the percentile ranks for raw scores of 33 and 76 from 50th to 99th.

These findings suggest that older adults are not as proficient as younger adults at tasks involving working memory, processing speed, perceptual organization, and the capacity to handle mental operations that involve nonverbal abstract reasoning. If we view the performance tasks as measures of fluid intelligence and the verbal tasks as measures of crystallized intelligence, then the WAIS–III age norms indicate that fluid abilities are not as well developed as crystallized abilities in older people. *These differences do not reflect changes in intelligence with age; rather, they only show how older adults compare with younger adults.* To study changes in intelligence with age, we would need to have longitudinal data to see how 80-year-olds, for example, functioned on these same tasks when they were 20-year-olds. Please note that, based on the WAIS–R, it is incorrect to conclude, as we did on page 224 of this text, that "fluid intelligence, but not crystallized intelligence, shows a marked decrement with advancing age." All we can say based on the WAIS–R or WAIS–III norms is that in some respects people of advanced age differ in ability from those who are younger. Recent longitudinal research on twins, however, does indicate that performance on Block Design declines steadily from 60 to 90 years, whereas there is little or no age-related change for Vocabulary (McArdle, Prescott, Hamagami, & Horn, 1998). These data support the hypothesis that fluid intelligence, but not crystallized intelligence, shows a marked decrement with advancing age.

ASSETS OF THE WAIS–III

The WAIS–III is a well-standardized test, with excellent reliability and good concurrent and construct validity. The 14 subtests are divided into a Verbal and a Performance section, and the test provides a Verbal, Performance, and Full Scale IQ. When the two supplementary subtests are administered in conjunction with the standard 11 subtests, the test also yields four index scores: Verbal Comprehension, Perceptual Organization, Working Memory, and Processing Speed. This procedure is helpful in clinical and psychoeducational work and in the assessment of brain-behavior relationships. A valuable feature of the test is that most examinees take a comparable battery of subtests. Parts of the test can be administered to examinees limited by sensory impairment (for example, the Verbal Scale may be given to blind individuals or to those with motor handicaps; the Performance Scale may be given to hard-of-hearing individuals). Here are some other assets of the WAIS–III.

1. *Excellent standardization.* The standardization procedures were excellent, sampling four geographical regions; both sexes; White, Black, Hispanic, and other racial/ethnic groups; and the entire socioeconomic status range. The standardization sample well represents the nation as a whole for the age groups covered by the test.

2. *Excellent overall psychometric properties.* The WAIS–III has excellent reliability for the IQs and Index scores. The studies in the *WAIS–III—WMS–III Technical Manual* indicate good concurrent and construct validity, although we need more research to evaluate the different forms of validity of the latest edition of the test; this is especially true of the Index scores.

3. *Good administration procedures.* The procedures described in the *WAIS–III Administration and Scoring Manual* are excellent. The examiner actively probes responses to evaluate the breadth of the examinee's knowledge and to determine whether the individual truly knows the answer. On items that require two reasons for maximum credit, examinees are asked for another reason when they give only one reason. These procedures ensure that the test does not penalize examinees for failing to understand the demands of the questions. The emphasis on probing questions and queries is extremely desirable. Also desirable is the inclusion of practice items on some subtests.

4. *Good manual.* The *WAIS–III Administration and Scoring Manual* is easy to use; it provides clear directions and tables. Examiners are aided by instructions printed in a different color from that of other text material. The manual provides helpful abbreviations for recording the examinee's responses, such as P for Pass, F for Fail, Q for Query/Question, DK for Don't Know, NR for No Response, Inc. for Incomplete, PC for Points Correctly, and PX for Points Incorrectly. The *WAIS–III—WMS–III Technical Manual* provides extensive information concerning the validity, reliability, and interpretation of the test.

5. *Helpful scoring criteria.* The criteria for scoring replies have been carefully prepared. The Vocabulary and Similarities scoring guidelines, for example, detail the rationale for 2-, 1-, and 0-point scores. Several examples demonstrate application of the scoring principles. Many typical responses are provided and scored, and those deemed to need further inquiry are indicated by a Q. Scoring criteria and sample responses for the Vocabulary, Comprehension, and Similarities subtests are placed with the subtest proper, rather than in appendixes in the back of the manual.

6. *Decreased reliance on timed performance.* Although speed of performance is important on the WAIS–III, the new Matrix Reasoning subtest has no time limits and the Object Assembly subtest, which relies heavily on bonus points for quick completion, is now an optional subtest and is not required for calculation of the IQ or Index scores. The number of bonus points possible for quick performance has been reduced on some subtests. The reduced time re-

quirements appear to be an asset in testing elderly examinees.

7. *Co-normed with an individual measure of memory and linked to a measure of academic achievement.* The WAIS–III was co-normed with the Wechsler Memory Scale–III (WMS–III; Wechsler, 1997) for all 13 age groups in the WAIS–III standardization sample. For persons in the age range 16–19 years, the WAIS–III was linked with the Wechsler Individual Achievement Test (WIAT; The Psychological Corporation, 1997). These procedures provide information about what scores to expect on the WMS–III and WIAT when you know the examinee's scores on the WAIS–III and vice versa.

LIMITATIONS OF THE WAIS–III

Although the WAIS–III is, overall, an excellent instrument, some problems do exist.

1. *Limited floor and ceiling.* The test is not applicable for severely retarded or extremely gifted individuals.

2. *Low reliability of three subtests.* Reliability coefficients for the Picture Arrangement, Symbol Search, and Object Assembly subtests are lower than .80 at most ages.

3. *Nonuniformity of subtest scaled scores.* Because the range of scaled scores is less than 19 on some subtests, there may be minor problems in profile analysis in some age groups at the lower and upper extremes of scores.

4. *Difficulty in interpreting norms when you substitute a supplementary subtest for a regular subtest.* With norms for the three IQs based on 11 standard subtests, there is no way of knowing precisely what scores mean when you substitute one of the supplementary subtests (Letter–Number Sequencing and Symbol Search) or the optional subtest (Object Assembly) for a regular subtest. You should make a substitution of this kind only in unusual circumstances and, when you report the results, label them "tentative."

5. *Possible difficulties in scoring responses.* Work with previous editions of the WAIS suggests that Similarities, Vocabulary, and Comprehension may be difficult to score. The *WAIS–III—WMS–III Technical Manual* cites a series of scoring studies in which there was high agreement among examiners in the scores they gave to these subtests (and to the Information subtest as well). These results are encouraging, but researchers need to replicate them. We recommend that you consult colleagues when you are having trouble scoring responses.

6. *Poor quality or design of some test materials.* The templates for scoring the Digit Symbol—Coding and Symbol Search subtests are poorly constructed and may tear and disintegrate quickly.

THINKING THROUGH THE ISSUES

In what situations would it be appropriate to administer the WAIS–III and in what situations would it be inappropriate to administer the WAIS–III?

How well do the items on the WAIS–III relate to everyday cognitive functions?

Which subtests on the WAIS–III do you like the most, and which ones do you like the least?

Do you believe that the WAIS–III is culturally biased? Explain your reasoning.

Why do you think some cognitive functions differ between older and younger people?

How would the WAIS–III assist in a vocational assessment?

How could the results of the WAIS–III be useful in rehabilitation programs?

How does the WAIS–III differ from the WISC–III? Compared to the WISC–III, what are some unique features of the WAIS–III?

Should the WAIS–III be considered a neuropsychological instrument? What is the basis for your answer?

Under what circumstances would you administer an abbreviated form of the WAIS–III? How might you decide which subtests to administer?

Do you think that the type of medication an examinee is taking can influence his or her WAIS–III performance? If so, what types of medications might you be concerned about?

If an examinee didn't sleep well the night before a WAIS–III examination, might this have an impact on her or his performance? What are some of the signs of excessive fatigue? What subtests might be affected adversely by excessive fatigue?

Is it possible for an examinee to fake cognitive problems on the WAIS–III? If so, in what assessment situations might faking be a potential problem?

Which WAIS–III subtest results might be most distorted by depression and by anxiety?

What are some clinical situations in which repeat testing with the WAIS–III would be an appropriate recommendation?

How can you relate theories of intelligence to the composition of the WAIS–III?

SUMMARY

1. The Psychological Corporation published the WAIS–III in 1997, 16 years after the former edition, the WAIS–R. The WAIS–III is similar to its predecessor, with more than 68 percent of the items retained, as well as the original Digit Symbol subtest, which was slightly modified. Matrix Reasoning, a standard subtest, and Letter–Number Sequencing and Symbol Search, two supplementary subtests, are new. The WAIS–III is applicable to adolescents and adults from 16-0-0 to 89-11-30 years of age. Standardization of the test was excellent and included White, Black, Hispanic, and other ethnic groups.

2. The WAIS–III provides Deviation IQs for the Verbal, Performance, and Full Scales ($M = 100$, $SD = 15$) and standard scores for the 14 subtests ($M = 10$, $SD = 3$).

3. The internal consistency reliabilities of the Verbal, Performance, and Full Scales are excellent (average r_{xx} of .97, .94, and .98, respectively). Average subtest internal consistency reliabilities range from .70 to .93, and average test-retest reliabilities range from .76 to .94. Reliabilities for the Verbal, Performance, and Full Scales are higher than those for the individual subtests.

4. Average standard errors of measurement are 2.55 for the Verbal Scale, 3.67 for the Performance Scale, and 2.30 for the Full Scale. The most confidence can be placed in the Full Scale, followed by the Verbal Scale and then the Performance Scale.

5. Increases in IQ produced by practice effects (after approximately a one-month interval) averaged from 3.2 to 5.7 points on the Full Scale,

2.0 to 3.2 points on the Verbal Scale, and 3.7 to 8.3 points on the Performance Scale.

6. Studies reported in the *WAIS–III—WMS–III Technical Manual* suggest that the WAIS–III has acceptable concurrent, criterion, and construct validity. Correlations between the Full Scale IQ and other measures of intelligence, achievement, and memory range from .64 to .93.

7. The *WAIS–III—WMS–III Technical Manual* indicates that the WAIS–III provides *lower* IQs than does the WAIS–R, by about 3 points, and higher scores than does the WISC–III, by about 1 point, in the overlapping ages.

8. The Verbal Scale subtests correlate more highly with each other ($Mdn\ r = .57$) than do the Performance Scale subtests ($Mdn\ r = .49$). Correlations between the Verbal subtests and the Verbal Scale ($Mdn\ r = .76$) are higher than those between the Performance subtests and the Performance Scale ($Mdn\ r = .64$). The Verbal subtests also have higher correlations with the Full Scale ($Mdn\ r = .75$) than do the Performance subtests ($Mdn\ r = .63$).

9. A factor analysis of the WAIS–III standardization data indicated that four factors account for the test's structure at most age groups: Verbal Comprehension, Perceptual Organization, Working Memory, and Processing Speed. The best measures of g are Vocabulary, Similarities, Information, Comprehension, Arithmetic, Block Design, and Matrix Reasoning.

10. Because several WAIS–III subtests have an adequate degree of subtest specificity, interpretation of profiles of subtest scores is on firm ground for these subtests.

11. The Index scores are formed by the following combinations of subtests: (a) Vocabulary, Similarities, and Information for Verbal Comprehension; (b) Picture Completion, Block Design, and Matrix Reasoning for Perceptual Organization; (c) Arithmetic, Digit Span, and Letter–Number Sequencing for Working Memory; and (d) Digit Symbol—Coding and Symbol Search for Processing Speed.

12. The subtest scaled-score range is 1 to 19, but not at all age groups. For some age groups and for some subtests, the highest attainable scaled score is 17. For persons in the age groups 80–84 years and 85–89 years, the lowest attainable scaled scores on the Picture Arrangement subtest are 4 and 5, respectively.

13. The WAIS–III does not adequately assess the cognitive ability of examinees who are either severely retarded or exceptionally gifted. The range of Full Scale IQs is 45 to 155.

14. The WAIS–III differs from the WAIS–R in several ways. The most noticeable changes are the addition of three new subtests (Letter–Number Sequencing, Matrix Reasoning, and Symbol Search), two new factors (Working Memory and Processing Speed), and full color for many of the pictures. Items have been added or changed on every subtest, and numerous administrative changes have been made.

15. Developing proper administrative procedures early in your testing and assessment career is an important step in becoming a competent clinician.

16. Examiners may make administrative errors. These include failing to follow the scoring rules, failing to complete the Record Form properly, failing to adhere to directions, failing to probe ambiguous responses, and failing to follow starting-point and discontinuance procedures.

17. Adequate hearing and language functions are required for the Verbal Scale subtests, and adequate vision and visual-motor ability are needed for the Performance Scale subtests. If you have any doubts about the examinee's auditory functions, language functions, visual functions, or motor functions, use screening procedures to determine whether the examinee has any deficits in these abilities.

18. You should follow the standard order of administering the subtests in all but the most exceptional circumstances.

19. Some examinees may not be able to complete the full battery of subtests in a single session. In such cases, schedule breaks to coincide with the end of a subtest so that testing can easily be resumed at a later time.

20. To ensure that scoring is standardized at the starting and discontinuance points, credit any items failed below the starting-point items when the examinee passes the starting-point items, and do not credit any items passed above the discontinuance-point items when the examinee fails the discontinuance-point items.

21. The WAIS–III requires the use of many probing questions and queries. Give spoiled responses a score of 0.

22. Because modifications in test procedures may increase the examinee's scores, use modifications only *after* the standard administration.

23. In any situation in which a basal level is not established, follow the discontinuance procedure for the subtest.

24. Short forms of the WAIS–III, although practical, have several disadvantages. Short-form IQs may be less stable, impede profile analysis, and result in misclassifications. Do not use short forms for any placement, educational, or clinical decision-making purpose. If you need to use a short form for screening purposes, follow the procedures advocated by Tellegen and Briggs to determine the Deviation IQs. Table O-6 in Appendix O shows the best short-form combinations of two, three, four, and five WAIS–III subtests. This table also shows short forms useful for rapid screening and for hard-of-hearing examinees. Tables O-7, O-8, O-9, and O-10 in Appendix O show estimated IQs associated with these short-form combinations. The best two-subtest short-form combination is Vocabulary and Matrix Reasoning. Table O-11 provides estimated IQs for one six-subtest short-form combination and two seven-subtest short-form combinations.

25. Although you can view the WISC–III and WAIS–III as alternative forms for examinees aged 16-0-0 to 16-11-30 years, we recommend that you give the WISC–III to examinees with below-average ability, either test to examinees with average ability, and the WAIS–III to examinees with above-average ability.

26. The assets of the WAIS–III include its excellent standardization, excellent reliability, adequate validity, good administrative procedures, and excellent test manuals. The test uses interesting materials and helpful scoring criteria, and there is extensive research and clinical literature based on prior editions.

27. The limitations of the WAIS–III include limited range of IQs (155 to 45), low reliability of some subtests, difficulty in interpreting norms when you substitute one or both supplementary subtests for standard subtests, difficulty in scoring some subtests, and poor quality of some test materials.

28. Overall, the WAIS–III represents a major contribution to the field of intelligence testing of adolescents and adults. It serves as an important instrument for this purpose.

KEY TERMS, CONCEPTS, AND NAMES

Wechsler-Bellevue Intelligence Scale (p. 1204)
WAIS–III standardization (p. 1204)
WAIS–III Deviation IQ (p. 1205)
WAIS–III scaled scores (p. 1206)
Prorating procedure (p. 1206)
Reliability of the WAIS–III (p. 1206)
Subtest reliabilities of the WAIS–III (p. 1206)
Standard errors of measurement of the WAIS–III
    (p. 1206)
Stability of the WAIS–III (p. 1207)
Changes in WAIS–III IQs (p. 1208)
Changes in WAIS–III subtest scores (p. 1209)
Confidence intervals for WAIS–III IQs (p. 1209)
Content validity of the WAIS–III (p. 1211)
Concurrent validity of the WAIS–III (p. 1211)
Construct validity of the WAIS–III (p. 1213)
WAIS–III subtest intercorrelations (p. 1213)
Factor analysis of the WAIS–III (p. 1214)
WAIS–III Verbal Comprehension factor
    (p. 1214)
WAIS–III Perceptual Organization factor
    (p. 1214)
WAIS–III Working Memory factor (p. 1215)
WAIS–III Processing Speed factor (p. 1215)
WAIS–III subtests as measures of g (p. 1215)
Subtest specificity on the WAIS–III (p. 1217)
WAIS–III Index scores (p. 1218)
Range of WAIS–III subtest scores (p. 1220)
Range of WAIS–III Full Scale IQs (p. 1220)
Comparison of WAIS–III and WAIS–R (p. 1221)
Administering the WAIS–III (p. 1222)
Physical abilities required for the WAIS–III
    (p. 1225)
Subtest sequence on the WAIS–III (p. 1236)
Starting rules on the WAIS–III (p. 1237)
Discontinuance rules on the WAIS–III (p. 1238)
Repetition of items on the WAIS–III (p. 1238)
Use of probing questions and queries on the
    WAIS–III (p. 1238)
Spoiled responses on the WAIS–III (p. 1238)
Modifying standard procedures on the WAIS–III
    (p. 1238)
WAIS–III short forms (p. 1239)
Satz-Mogel abbreviated procedure for the WAIS–III
    (p. 1240)
WAIS–III Vocabulary (p. 1243)
WAIS–III Similarities (p. 1243)
WAIS–III Arithmetic (p. 1244)

WAIS–III Digit Span (p. 1244)
WAIS–III Comprehension (p. 1246)
WAIS–III Letter–Number Sequencing (p. 1246)
WAIS–III Picture Completion (p. 1247)
WAIS–III Digit Symbol—Coding (p. 1248)
WAIS–III Block Design (p. 1249)
WAIS–III Matrix Reasoning (p. 1250)
WAIS–III Picture Arrangement (p. 1251)
WAIS–III Symbol Search (p. 1251)
WAIS–III Object Assembly (p. 1252)
Interpreting the WAIS–III (p. 1252)
Profile analysis of the WAIS–III (p. 1252)
Base rate Verbal-Performance IQ differences
    (p. 1253)
Statistically reliable vs. empirically observed IQ
    differences (p. 1256)
Age and WAIS–III subtest performance (p. 1257)
Assets of the WAIS–III (p. 1259)
Limitations of the WAIS–III (p. 1260)

STUDY QUESTIONS

1. Discuss the following topics with respect to the WAIS–III: standardization, Deviation IQs, scaled scores, reliability, and validity.

2. Describe and interpret WAIS–III factor analytic findings.

3. Discuss important factors involved in administering the WAIS–III.

4. Discuss WAIS–III short forms, including their value and limitations.

5. Discuss the rationale, factor analytic findings, reliability and correlational highlights, and administrative and interpretive considerations for each of the WAIS–III subtests: Vocabulary, Similarities, Arithmetic, Digit Span, Information, Comprehension, Letter–Number Sequencing, Picture Completion, Digit Symbol—Coding, Block Design, Matrix Reasoning, Picture Arrangement, Symbol Search, and Object Assembly.

6. Discuss the intent of profile analysis, methods of profile analysis, and approaches to profile analysis on the WAIS–III.

7. Discuss the assets and limitations of the WAIS–III.

APPENDIX O

TABLES FOR THE WAIS-III

O-1. Confidence Intervals for WAIS–III Scales and Index Scores Based on Obtained Score Only   1266

O-2. Significant Differences Between WAIS–III Scaled Scores, IQs, and Index Scores for Ages 16–17, 18–19, and for the Average of the 13 Age Groups (.05/.01 significance levels)   1269

O-3. Differences Required for Significance When Each WAIS–III Subtest Scaled Score Is Compared to the Mean Subtest Scaled Score for an Individual Examinee 1270

O-4. Estimates of Probability of Obtaining Designated Differences Between Individual WAIS–III Verbal and Performance IQs by Chance   1272

O-5. Estimates of the Probability of Obtaining Designated Differences Between Individual WAIS–III Index Score Deviation Quotients (DQs) by Chance 1273

O-6. Reliability and Validity Coefficients of Proposed WAIS–III Short Forms   1274

O-7. Estimated WAIS–III Full Scale Deviation Quotients for Sum of Scaled Scores for Ten Best Short-Form Dyads and Other Combinations   1275

O-8. Estimated WAIS–III Full Scale Deviation Quotients for Sum of Scaled Scores for Ten Best Short-Form Triads and Other Combinations   1277

O-9. Estimated WAIS–III Full Scale Deviation Quotients for Sum of Scaled Scores for Ten Best Short-Form Tetrads and Other Combinations   1279

O-10. Estimated WAIS–III Full Scale Deviation Quotients for Sum of Scaled Scores for Ten Best Short-Form Pentads and Other Combinations   1281

O-11. Estimated WAIS–III Full Scale Deviation Quotients for Sum of Scaled Scores for One Six-Subtest Short-Form Combination and Two Seven-Subtest Short-Form Combinations   1283

Table O-1
Confidence Intervals for WAIS–III Scales and Index Scores Based on Obtained Score Only

Age group	Scale	Confidence level				
		68%	85%	90%	95%	99%
16–17	Verbal Scale IQ	± 3	± 5	± 5	± 6	± 8
	Performance Scale IQ	± 5	± 6	± 7	± 8	±11
	Full Scale IQ	± 3	± 4	± 5	± 6	± 7
	Verbal Comprehension	± 4	± 6	± 6	± 8	±10
	Perceptual Organization	± 5	± 6	± 7	± 8	±11
	Working Memory	± 4	± 6	± 7	± 8	±11
	Processing Speed	± 6	± 8	±10	±11	±15
18–19	Verbal Scale IQ	± 3	± 4	± 5	± 5	± 7
	Performance Scale IQ	± 5	± 6	± 7	± 9	±11
	Full Scale IQ	± 3	± 4	± 4	± 5	± 7
	Verbal Comprehension	± 4	± 5	± 6	± 7	± 9
	Perceptual Organization	± 5	± 7	± 8	± 9	±12
	Working Memory	± 4	± 5	± 6	± 7	± 9
	Processing Speed	± 6	± 8	±10	±11	±15
20–24	Verbal Scale IQ	± 3	± 4	± 5	± 6	± 7
	Performance Scale IQ	± 4	± 6	± 7	± 8	±10
	Full Scale IQ	± 3	± 4	± 4	± 5	± 7
	Verbal Comprehension	± 4	± 5	± 6	± 7	± 9
	Perceptual Organization	± 4	± 6	± 7	± 8	±10
	Working Memory	± 4	± 6	± 7	± 8	±11
	Processing Speed	± 6	± 9	±10	±11	±15
25–29	Verbal Scale IQ	± 3	± 4	± 5	± 5	± 7
	Performance Scale IQ	± 4	± 5	± 6	± 7	± 9
	Full Scale IQ	± 3	± 4	± 4	± 5	± 6
	Verbal Comprehension	± 4	± 5	± 6	± 6	± 8
	Perceptual Organization	± 4	± 5	± 6	± 7	± 9
	Working Memory	± 4	± 6	± 7	± 8	±11
	Processing Speed	± 6	± 8	± 9	±11	±15
30–34	Verbal Scale IQ	± 3	± 4	± 5	± 5	± 7
	Performance Scale IQ	± 4	± 6	± 7	± 8	±11
	Full Scale IQ	± 3	± 4	± 4	± 5	± 6
	Verbal Comprehension	± 3	± 5	± 5	± 6	± 8
	Perceptual Organization	± 5	± 6	± 7	± 8	±11
	Working Memory	± 4	± 6	± 7	± 8	±10
	Processing Speed	± 5	± 8	± 9	±10	±13
35–44	Verbal Scale IQ	± 3	± 4	± 5	± 5	± 7
	Performance Scale IQ	± 4	± 6	± 6	± 7	±10
	Full Scale IQ	± 3	± 4	± 4	± 5	± 6
	Verbal Comprehension	± 4	± 5	± 5	± 6	± 8
	Perceptual Organization	± 4	± 6	± 7	± 8	±10
	Working Memory	± 4	± 6	± 7	± 8	±10
	Processing Speed	± 5	± 8	± 9	±10	±13

(Continued)

Table O-1 (*Continued*)

Age group	Scale	Confidence level				
		68%	85%	90%	95%	99%
45–54	Verbal Scale IQ	± 3	± 4	± 5	± 5	± 7
	Performance Scale IQ	± 4	± 6	± 6	± 7	±10
	Full Scale IQ	± 3	± 4	± 4	± 5	± 6
	Verbal Comprehension	± 4	± 5	± 5	± 6	± 8
	Perceptual Organization	± 4	± 6	± 7	± 8	±11
	Working Memory	± 4	± 6	± 6	± 7	±10
	Processing Speed	± 5	± 7	± 8	±10	±13
55–64	Verbal Scale IQ	± 3	± 4	± 4	± 5	± 7
	Performance Scale IQ	± 4	± 5	± 6	± 7	± 9
	Full Scale IQ	± 3	± 3	± 4	± 5	± 6
	Verbal Comprehension	± 3	± 4	± 5	± 6	± 8
	Perceptual Organization	± 4	± 5	± 6	± 7	± 9
	Working Memory	± 4	± 6	± 7	± 8	±10
	Processing Speed	± 5	± 7	± 8	±10	±13
65–69	Verbal Scale IQ	± 3	± 4	± 4	± 5	± 6
	Performance Scale IQ	± 4	± 5	± 5	± 6	± 8
	Full Scale IQ	± 2	± 3	± 4	± 4	± 5
	Verbal Comprehension	± 3	± 4	± 5	± 6	± 7
	Perceptual Organization	± 4	± 5	± 6	± 7	± 9
	Working Memory	± 4	± 6	± 7	± 8	±10
	Processing Speed	± 5	± 7	± 8	±10	±13
70–74	Verbal Scale IQ	± 3	± 4	± 5	± 5	± 7
	Performance Scale IQ	± 4	± 5	± 6	± 7	± 9
	Full Scale IQ	± 3	± 4	± 4	± 5	± 6
	Verbal Comprehension	± 4	± 5	± 6	± 7	± 9
	Perceptual Organization	± 4	± 6	± 7	± 8	±10
	Working Memory	± 4	± 6	± 6	± 7	±10
	Processing Speed	± 5	± 8	± 9	±10	±13
75–79	Verbal Scale IQ	± 3	± 4	± 5	± 6	± 7
	Performance Scale IQ	± 5	± 6	± 7	± 8	±11
	Full Scale IQ	± 3	± 4	± 5	± 5	± 7
	Verbal Comprehension	± 3	± 5	± 5	± 6	± 8
	Perceptual Organization	± 5	± 7	± 8	± 9	±12
	Working Memory	± 5	± 7	± 8	± 9	±12
	Processing Speed	± 6	± 8	± 9	±10	±14
80–84	Verbal Scale IQ	± 3	± 4	± 5	± 5	± 7
	Performance Scale IQ	± 4	± 6	± 6	± 8	±10
	Full Scale IQ	± 3	± 4	± 4	± 5	± 6
	Verbal Comprehension	± 3	± 4	± 5	± 6	± 8
	Perceptual Organization	± 5	± 6	± 7	± 9	±11
	Working Memory	± 4	± 6	± 7	± 8	±10
	Processing Speed	± 6	± 8	± 9	±10	±14

(*Continued*)

Table O-1 (*Continued*)

Age group	Scale	Confidence level				
		68%	85%	90%	95%	99%
85–89	Verbal Scale IQ	± 4	± 5	± 6	± 6	± 8
	Performance Scale IQ	± 4	± 6	± 7	± 8	±10
	Full Scale IQ	± 3	± 4	± 5	± 6	± 7
	Verbal Comprehension	± 3	± 5	± 5	± 6	± 8
	Perceptual Organization	± 5	± 7	± 8	±10	±13
	Working Memory	± 5	± 7	± 8	± 9	±12
	Processing Speed	± 6	± 8	± 9	±10	±13
Average	Verbal Scale IQ	± 3	± 4	± 5	± 5	± 7
	Performance Scale IQ	± 4	± 6	± 7	± 8	±10
	Full Scale IQ	± 3	± 4	± 4	± 5	± 6
	Verbal Comprehension	± 4	± 5	± 5	± 6	± 8
	Perceptual Organization	± 4	± 6	± 7	± 8	±11
	Working Memory	± 4	± 6	± 7	± 8	±10
	Processing Speed	± 6	± 8	± 9	±11	±14

Note. See Table C-1 (page 813) for an explanation of the method used to obtain confidence intervals. Confidence intervals in this table were obtained by using the appropriate SE_m located in Table 3.4 (p. 54) in the *WAIS–III—WMS–III Technical Manual.*

Table O-2
Significant Differences Between WAIS–III Scaled Scores, IQs, and Index Scores for Ages 16–17, for Ages 18–19, and for the Average of the 13 Age Groups (.05/.01 significance levels)

	V	S	A	DS	I	C	LN	PC	CD	BD	MR	PA	SS

Ages 16–17

	V	S	A	DS	I	C	LN	PC	CD	BD	MR	PA	SS
S	4/5												
A	3/4	4/5											
DS	3/4	4/5	3/4										
I	3/4	4/5	3/4	3/4									
C	3/4	4/5	4/5	3/4	4/5								
LN	4/5	4/6	4/5	4/5	4/5	4/5							
PC	4/5	4/5	4/5	4/5	4/5	4/5	4/6						
CD	4/5	4/5	4/5	4/5	4/5	4/5	4/5	4/5					
BD	3/4	4/5	3/4	3/4	3/4	4/5	4/5	4/5	4/5				
MR	3/4	4/5	3/4	3/4	3/4	4/5	5/6	4/5	4/5	3/4			
PA	4/5	5/6	4/6	4/5	4/5	4/6	5/6	5/6	5/6	4/6	4/6		
SS	4/5	4/6	4/5	4/5	4/5	4/6	5/6	4/6	4/6	4/5	4/5	5/6	
OA	4/5	4/6	4/5	4/5	4/5	4/6	5/6	4/6	4/6	4/5	4/5	5/6	5/6

PSIQ vs VSIQ: 10/13

	VCDQ	WMDQ	PSDQ
PODQ	11/14	12/15	14/18
WMDQ	11/14	—	14/18
PSDQ	13/18	14/18	—

Ages 18–19

	V	S	A	DS	I	C	LN	PC	CD	BD	MR	PA	SS
S	3/4												
A	3/4	4/5											
DS	3/4	3/4	3/4										
I	3/4	3/4	3/4	3/4									
C	3/4	4/5	3/4	3/4	3/4								
LN	3/4	4/5	3/4	3/4	3/4	3/4							
PC	4/5	4/5	4/5	4/5	4/5	4/5	4/5						
CD	3/4	4/5	4/5	4/5	4/5	4/5	4/5	4/6					
BD	3/4	4/5	3/4	3/4	3/4	3/4	3/4	4/5	4/5				
MR	3/4	3/4	3/4	3/4	3/4	3/4	3/4	4/5	4/5	3/4			
PA	4/5	4/6	4/5	4/5	4/5	4/6	4/5	5/6	5/6	4/5	4/5		
SS	4/5	4/5	4/5	4/8	4/5	4/5	4/5	5/6	4/6	4/5	4/5	5/6	
OA	4/5	4/6	4/6	4/5	4/5	4/6	4/6	5/6	5/6	4/6	4/5	5/6	5/6

PSIQ vs VSIQ: 10/13

	VCDQ	WMDQ	PSDQ
PODQ	11/14	11/15	14/19
WMDQ	9/12	—	13/17
PSDQ	13/17	13/17	—

Average of 13 age groups

	V	S	A	DS	I	C	LN	PC	CD	BD	MR	PA	SS
S	3/4												
A	3/4	3/4											
DS	3/4	3/4	3/4										
I	3/4	3/4	3/4	3/4									
C	3/4	4/5	4/5	3/4	3/4								
LN	3/4	4/5	4/5	4/5	4/5	4/5							
PC	3/4	4/5	4/5	4/5	4/4	4/5	4/5						
CD	3/4	4/5	4/5	4/5	3/4	4/5	4/5	4/5					
BD	3/4	4/5	4/4	3/4	3/4	4/5	4/5	4/5	4/5				
MR	3/4	3/4	3/4	3/4	3/4	4/4	4/5	4/5	3/4	3/4			
PA	4/5	4/5	4/5	4/5	4/5	4/6	4/6	4/6	4/5	4/5	4/5		
SS	4/5	4/5	4/5	4/5	4/5	4/5	4/5	4/5	4/5	4/5	4/5	5/6	
OA	4/5	4/6	4/6	4/5	4/5	5/6	5/6	5/6	4/6	4/6	4/5	5/6	5/6

PSIQ vs VSIQ: 9/12

	VCDQ	WMDQ	PSDQ
PODQ	10/13	11/15	13/17
WMDQ	10/13	—	13/17
PSDQ	12/16	13/17	—

Note. Abbreviations: V = Vocabulary, S = Similarities, A = Arithmetic, DS = Digit Span, I = Information, C = Comprehension, LN = Letter–Number Sequencing, PC = Picture Completion, CD = Digit Symbol—Coding, BD = Block Design, MR = Matrix Reasoning, PA = Picture Arrangement, SS = Symbol Search, OA = Object Assembly, VSIQ = Verbal Scale IQ, PSIQ = Performance Scale IQ, VCDQ = Verbal Comprehension Deviation Quotient, PODQ = Perceptual Organization Deviation Quotient, WMDQ = Working Memory Deviation Quotient, PSDQ = Processing Speed Deviation Quotient.

The factor scores are composed of the following subtests: Verbal Comprehension: Vocabulary, Similarities, Information; Perceptual Organization: Picture Completion, Block Design, Matrix Reasoning; Working Memory: Arithmetic, Digit Span, Letter–Number Sequencing; Processing Speed: Digit Symbol—Coding, Symbol Search.

Sample reading: A difference of 4 points between scaled scores on the Vocabulary and Similarities is significant at the 5 percent level; a difference of 5 points is significant at the 1 percent level. The first small box shows that a 10-point difference between the Verbal Scale IQ and the Performance Scale IQ is needed at the 5 percent level, and a 13-point difference is needed at the 1 percent level. The second small box shows that a difference of 11 points is needed between the Verbal Comprehension Deviation Quotient and the Perceptual Organization Deviation Quotient at the 5 percent level, and a difference of 14 points is needed at the 1 percent level. The other comparisons between Deviation Quotients are read in a similar manner.

The values in this table for the subtest comparisons are overly liberal when more than one comparison is made for a subtest. They are more accurate when a priori planned comparisons are made, such as Information vs. Comprehension or Digit Span vs. Arithmetic.

All values in this table have been rounded to the next higher number.

See Chapter 8, Exhibit 8-1 (page 168) for an explanation of the method used to arrive at the magnitudes of differences.

See Exhibit I-4 (pages 1069–1070) in Appendix I for the procedure used to obtain the reliability coefficients for the factor scores.

Table O-3
Differences Required for Significance When Each WAIS–III Subtest Scaled Score Is Compared to the Mean Subtest Scaled Score for an Individual Examinee

	Average of all age groups											
	Mean of 2 subtests		Mean of 3 subtests[a]		Mean of 3 subtests		Mean of 5 subtests		Mean of 6 subtests[b]		Mean of 6 subtests	
Subtest	.05	.01	.05	.01	.05	.01	.05	.01	.05	.01	.05	.01
Vocabulary	—	—	1.70	2.09	—	—	—	—	2.02	2.41	2.06	2.45
Similarities	—	—	2.03	2.48	—	—	—	—	2.65	3.15	2.68	3.19
Arithmetic	—	—	—	—	2.11	2.58	—	—	2.51	2.99	2.54	3.03
Digit Span	—	—	—	—	2.00	2.46	—	—	2.30	2.74	—	—
Information	—	—	1.82	2.23	—	—	—	—	2.24	2.67	2.28	2.71
Comprehension	—	—	—	—	—	—	—	—	2.83	3.36	2.85	3.40
Letter–Number Seq.	—	—	—	—	2.36	2.89	—	—	—	—	3.03	3.61
Picture Completion	—	—	2.32	2.85	—	—	2.87	3.44	3.02	3.59	3.04	3.62
Digit Symbol—Coding	2.08	2.61	—	—	—	—	2.77	3.32	2.91	3.46	2.93	3.48
Block Design	—	—	2.21	2.71	—	—	2.68	3.21	2.81	3.34	2.83	3.37
Matrix Reasoning	—	—	2.05	2.51	—	—	2.40	2.88	2.50	2.97	2.52	3.00
Picture Arrangement	—	—	—	—	—	—	3.37	4.04	3.57	4.24	3.59	4.27
Symbol Search	2.08	2.61	—	—	—	—	—	—	3.37	4.01	—	—
Object Assembly	—	—	—	—	—	—	—	—	—	—	3.85	4.58

	Mean of 7 subtests[c]		Mean of 11 subtests		Mean of 11 subtests		Mean of 11 subtests		Mean of 11 subtests		Mean of 12 subtests	
Subtest	.05	.01	.05	.01	.05	.01	.05	.01	.05	.01	.05	.01
Vocabulary	2.09	2.48	2.24	2.62	2.26	2.64	2.25	2.63	2.26	2.65	2.27	2.64
Similarities	2.76	3.28	3.03	3.54	3.04	3.55	3.04	3.55	3.05	3.56	3.08	3.59
Arithmetic	2.66	3.11	2.86	3.35	2.87	3.36	2.87	3.35	2.88	3.36	2.91	3.38
Digit Span	2.39	2.84	2.60	3.04	—	—	2.61	3.05	—	—	2.64	3.07
Information	2.33	2.72	2.53	2.95	2.54	2.96	2.53	2.96	2.54	2.97	2.56	2.98
Comprehension	2.95	3.50	3.25	3.80	3.26	3.81	3.26	3.81	3.27	3.82	3.31	3.85
Letter–Number Seq.	3.15	3.72	—	—	3.48	4.07	—	—	3.49	4.08	3.53	4.11
Picture Completion	3.15	3.73	3.25	3.92	3.36	3.93	3.36	3.92	3.36	3.93	3.41	3.96
Digit Symbol—Coding	3.02	3.59	3.20	3.74	3.21	3.75	—	—	—	—	3.26	3.79
Block Design	2.92	3.47	3.08	3.60	3.09	3.61	3.09	3.61	3.10	3.62	3.13	3.64
Matrix Reasoning	2.59	3.07	2.67	3.12	2.68	3.13	2.68	3.13	2.69	3.14	2.71	3.15
Picture Arrangement	3.73	4.43	4.05	4.73	4.05	4.74	4.05	4.73	4.06	4.74	4.12	4.79
Symbol Search	3.52	4.17	—	—	—	—	2.80	4.44	3.81	4.45	—	—
Object Assembly	4.01	4.75	—	—	—	—	—	—	—	—	—	—

(Continued)

Table O-3 (*Continued*)

Subtest	Mean of 12 subtests		Mean of 12 subtests		Mean of 13 subtests		Mean of 13 subtests		Mean of 13 subtests		Mean of 14 subtests	
	.05	.01	.05	.01	.05	.01	.05	.01	.05	.01	.05	.01
Vocabulary	2.28	2.65	2.29	2.66	2.30	2.67	2.30	2.68	2.31	2.68	2.33	2.69
Similarities	3.08	3.59	3.09	3.60	3.12	3.63	3.12	3.63	3.13	3.64	3.17	3.66
Arithmetic	2.91	3.39	2.92	3.39	2.94	3.42	2.95	3.43	2.95	3.43	2.99	3.45
Digit Span	2.64	3.07	2.65	3.08	2.67	3.10	2.67	3.11	2.68	3.11	2.71	3.13
Information	2.57	2.99	2.57	3.00	2.59	3.01	2.60	3.02	2.60	3.02	2.63	3.04
Comprehension	3.31	3.85	3.32	3.86	3.35	3.89	3.35	3.90	3.36	3.90	3.40	3.93
Letter–Number Seq.	—	—	—	—	3.58	4.16	3.58	4.17	—	—	3.64	4.20
Picture Completion	3.41	3.97	3.42	3.98	3.45	4.01	3.46	4.02	3.46	4.02	3.51	4.05
Digit Symbol—Coding	3.26	3.79	3.27	3.80	3.30	3.83	3.30	3.84	3.30	3.84	3.35	3.87
Block Design	3.13	3.65	3.14	3.65	3.17	3.69	3.18	3.69	3.18	3.69	3.22	3.72
Matrix Reasoning	2.71	3.16	2.72	3.17	2.74	3.19	2.75	3.19	2.75	3.20	2.78	3.21
Picture Arrangement	4.12	4.79	4.12	4.80	4.17	4.85	4.18	4.86	4.18	4.86	4.24	4.89
Symbol Search	3.86	4.50	—	—	3.91	4.55	—	—	3.92	4.56	3.98	4.59
Object Assembly	—	—	4.46	5.19	—	—	4.51	5.25	4.52	5.25	4.58	5.29

Note. This table shows the minimum deviations from an individual's average subtest scaled score that are significant at the .05 and .01 levels. See the Note to Table C-3 (page 815) for an explanation of the method used to obtain the deviations.

[a] In this column, the entries for Vocabulary, Similarities, and Arithmetic are compared to the mean of these three subtests. Similarly, the entries for Picture Completion, Block Design, and Matrix Reasoning are compared to the mean of these three subtests.

[b] In this column, the entries for Vocabulary, Similarities, Arithmetic, Digit Span, Information, and Comprehension are compared to the mean of these six subtests. Similarly, the entries for Picture Completion, Digit Symbol—Coding, Block Design, Matrix Reasoning, Picture Arrangement, and Symbol Search are compared to the mean of these six subtests.

[c] In this column, the entries for Vocabulary, Similarities, Arithmetic, Digit Span, Information, Comprehension, and Letter–Number Sequencing are compared to the mean of these seven subtests. Similarly, the entries for Picture Completion, Digit Symbol—Coding, Block Design, Matrix Reasoning, Picture Arrangement, Symbol Search, and Object Assembly are compared to the mean of these seven subtests.

Table O-4
Estimates of Probability of Obtaining Designated Differences Between Individual WAIS–III Verbal and Performance IQs by Chance

Probability of obtaining given or greater discrepancy by chance	Age group													Av.[a]
	16–17	18–19	20–24	25–29	30–34	35–44	45–54	55–64	65–69	70–74	75–79	80–84	85–89	
.50	3.31	3.21	3.10	2.82	3.12	2.89	2.90	2.70	2.48	2.84	3.22	2.96	3.24	2.99
.25	5.69	5.51	5.32	4.85	5.36	4.96	4.97	4.63	4.26	4.88	5.52	5.07	5.57	5.14
.20	6.33	6.13	5.92	5.40	5.97	5.53	5.53	5.15	4.74	5.43	6.14	5.65	6.20	5.72
.10	8.16	7.90	7.63	6.95	7.69	7.12	7.13	6.64	6.11	7.00	7.92	7.28	7.99	7.37
.05	9.70	9.39	9.06	8.26	9.14	8.46	8.47	7.89	7.26	8.32	9.41	8.65	9.49	8.76
.02	11.53	11.16	10.77	9.82	10.86	10.06	10.07	9.38	8.63	9.89	11.18	10.28	11.28	10.41
.01	12.76	12.35	11.93	10.88	12.03	11.14	11.15	10.39	9.56	10.95	12.38	11.38	12.49	11.53
.001	16.28	15.75	15.21	13.87	15.34	14.20	14.22	13.25	12.19	13.96	15.79	14.51	15.93	14.70

Note. Enter the table in the column appropriate to the examinee's age. Locate the discrepancy that is just less than the discrepancy obtained by the examinee. The entry in the first column in the same row gives the probability of obtaining a given or greater discrepancy by chance. For example, the probability that a 16-year-old examinee obtained a Verbal-Performance discrepancy of 12 by chance is estimated to be less than 2 percent. The table is two-tailed. See Chapter 8, Exhibit 8-1 (page 168) for an explanation of the method used to arrive at the magnitudes of differences.
[a] Av. = Average of the 13 age groups.

Table O-5
Estimates of the Probability of Obtaining Designated Differences Between Individual WAIS–III Index Score Deviation Quotients (DQs) by Chance

Probability of obtaining given or greater discrepancy by chance	Verbal Comprehension DQ vs. Perceptual Organization DQ	Verbal Comprehension DQ vs. Processing Speed DQ	Verbal Comprehension DQ vs. Working Memory DQ	Perceptual Organization DQ vs. Processing Speed DQ	Perceptual Organization DQ vs. Working Memory DQ	Processing Speed DQ vs. Working Memory DQ
.50	3.33	3.99	3.27	4.34	3.69	4.29
.25	5.71	6.84	5.61	7.45	6.34	7.37
.20	6.36	7.61	6.25	8.29	7.05	8.20
.10	8.19	9.81	8.05	10.68	9.09	10.57
.05	9.73	11.66	9.56	12.69	10.80	12.56
.02	11.57	13.86	11.37	15.09	12.84	14.93
.01	12.81	15.35	12.59	16.70	14.21	16.53
.001	16.34	19.57	16.05	21.30	18.12	21.08

Note. The values in this table are based on the total group. Locate the discrepancy that is just less than the discrepancy obtained by the examinee. The entry in the first column in the same row gives the probability of obtaining a given or greater discrepancy by chance. For example, the probability that an examinee obtained a Verbal Comprehension–Perceptual Organization discrepancy of 10 by chance is estimated to be 5 percent. The table is two-tailed. See Chapter 8, Exhibit 8-1 (page 168) for an explanation of the method used to arrive at the magnitudes of the differences.

Table O-6
Reliability and Validity Coefficients of Proposed WAIS–III Short Forms

Dyad

Short form	r_{tt}	r
V MR	.945	.881
V BD	.930	.876
V A	.941	.875
I MR[a,b]	.938	.867
I BD	.922	.865
S A	.917	.863
S MR	.922	.861
C MR	.914	.856
V I	.955	.853
V S	.940	.853
A PC[a]	.911	.836
A MR[a]	.930	.830
A PC[a]	.896	.829
I CD[a]	.909	.824
BD MR[b]	.925	.790
PC MR[a,b]	.909	.787
PC BD[b]	.899	.780
CD MR[b]	.907	.774
PC CD[a,b]	.881	.733
DS LN[c]	.911	.729
CD SS[d]	.882	.727
V S	.932	.852
BD CD	.894	.763
I A	.936	.850

Triad

Short form			r_{tt}	r
V	I	BD	.954	.906
V	A	PC	.939	.906
V	A	MR	.955	.905
V	A	BD	.947	.905
V	I	MR	.961	.905
V	A	PA	.927	.904
V	S	MR	.954	.902
S	I	MR	.950	.900
V	C	BD	.947	.899
V	S	MR[a]	.950	.899
A	I	MR[a]	.952	.891
A	PC	PC[a]	.936	.891
I	PC	MR[a]	.939	.887
I	CD	MR[a]	.938	.886
CD	BD	MR[b]	.931	.834
PC	BD	MR[b]	.934	.832
PC	CD	MR[b]	.922	.830
PC	CD	BD[b]	.917	.810
I	S	DS	.945	.882
V	S	I[e]	.960	.871
A	DS	LN[f]	.936	.820

Tetrad

Short form				r_{tt}	r
V	I	BD	MR	.963	.922
V	A	PC	MR	.955	.921
V	S	A	MR	.962	.920
V	A	BD	PA	.942	.920
V	S	A	BD	.957	.919
V	S	A	PC	.953	.919
V	A	I	BD	.962	.919
V	DS	PC	MR	.959	.918
V	S	A	BD	.950	.918
V	A	S	PA	.946	.912
A	I	PC	MR[a]	.953	.911
DS	I	PC	MR[a]	.950	.905
A	I	CD	MR[a]	.953	.904
A	CD	PC	CD[a]	.942	.900
PC	CD	BD	MR[b]	.941	.855
I	A	DS	S	.957	.899
I	S	CD	LN	.941	.918
MR	PC	CD	SS	.933	.865
I	A	PC	BD	.948	.907

Pentad

Short form					r_{tt}	r
V	A	I	PC	MR	.965	.934
V	S	A	PC	MR	.962	.935
V	A	C	PC	MR	.961	.933
V	S	A	BD	PA	.954	.933
V	DS	—	BD	MR	.967	.933
V	A	I	PC	BD	.962	.932
V	DS	—	PC	MR	.964	.932
V	I	CD	BD	MR	.963	.932
V	A	C	BD	PA	.953	.932
V	A	—	BD	PA	.958	.932
A	I	PC	PC	MR[a]	.955	.921
DS	I	—	PC	MR[a]	.960	.920
A	DS	—	CD	MR[a]	.953	.915
A	DS	—	PC	CD[a]	.960	.909

Note. The first 10 combinations represent the best ones based on validity. See Exhibit I-4 (page 1069) for formulas used to obtain reliability and validity coefficients.

[a] This combination is useful for rapid screening.

[b] This combination is useful for examinees who are hard-of-hearing.

[c] This combination provides an estimate of the Working Memory Index score.

[d] This combination provides an estimate of the Processing Speed Index score.

[e] This combination represents the subtests in the Verbal Comprehension Index.

[f] This combination represents the subtests in the Working Memory Index.

Table O-7
Estimated WAIS–III Full Scale Deviation Quotients for Sum of Scaled Scores for Ten Best Short-Form Dyads and Other Combinations

Sum of scaled scores	Combination													
	C2	C3	C4	C5	C6	C7	C8	C9	C10	C11	C12	C13	C14	C15
2	46	47	48	48	48	49	49	49	49	50	50	50	51	52
3	49	50	51	51	51	51	52	52	52	52	53	53	54	55
4	52	53	54	54	54	54	54	55	55	55	56	56	57	57
5	55	56	56	57	57	57	57	58	58	58	58	59	59	60
6	58	59	59	60	60	60	60	60	61	61	61	61	62	63
7	61	62	62	62	63	63	63	63	63	64	64	64	65	65
8	64	65	65	65	66	66	66	66	66	66	67	67	67	68
9	67	68	68	68	68	69	69	69	69	69	70	70	70	71
10	70	71	71	71	71	71	72	72	72	72	72	72	73	73
11	73	74	74	74	74	74	74	75	75	75	75	75	76	76
12	76	77	77	77	77	77	77	77	77	78	78	78	78	79
13	79	80	80	80	80	80	80	80	80	80	81	81	81	81
14	82	82	83	83	83	83	83	83	83	83	83	83	84	84
15	85	85	85	86	86	86	86	86	86	86	86	86	86	87
16	88	88	88	88	89	89	89	89	89	89	89	89	89	89
17	91	91	91	91	91	91	91	92	92	92	92	92	92	92
18	84	94	94	94	94	94	94	94	94	94	94	94	95	95
19	97	97	97	97	97	97	97	97	97	97	97	97	97	97
20	100	100	100	100	100	100	100	100	100	100	100	100	100	100
21	103	103	103	103	103	103	103	103	103	103	103	103	103	103
22	106	106	106	106	106	106	106	106	106	106	106	106	105	105
23	109	109	109	109	109	109	109	108	108	108	108	108	108	108
24	112	112	112	112	111	111	111	111	111	111	111	111	111	111
25	115	115	115	114	114	114	114	114	114	114	114	114	114	113
26	118	118	117	117	117	117	117	117	117	117	117	117	116	116
27	121	120	120	120	120	120	120	120	120	120	119	119	119	119
28	124	123	123	123	123	123	123	123	123	122	122	122	122	121
29	127	126	126	126	126	126	126	125	125	125	125	125	124	124
30	130	129	129	129	129	129	128	128	128	128	128	128	127	127
31	133	132	132	132	132	131	131	131	131	131	130	130	130	129
32	136	135	135	135	134	134	134	134	134	134	133	133	133	132
33	139	138	138	138	137	137	137	137	137	136	136	136	135	135
34	142	141	141	140	140	140	140	140	139	139	139	139	138	137
35	145	144	144	143	143	143	143	142	142	142	142	141	141	140
36	148	147	146	146	146	146	146	145	145	145	144	144	143	143
37	151	150	149	149	149	149	148	148	148	148	147	147	146	145
38	154	153	152	152	152	151	151	151	151	150	150	150	149	148

(Continued)

Table O-7 (*Continued*)

Note. The subtest combinations in each column are as follows:

C2 = I + CD[a]	C5 = V + BD[c]	C10 = A + MR[a]
BD + CD[b]	C6 = C + MR[c]	C11 = V + A[c]
A + PC[a]	PC + BD[b]	BD + MR[b]
PC + CD[a,b]	C7 = I + MR[d]	C12 = I + A
CD + MR[b]	C8 = S + MR[c]	C13 = CD + SS[f]
C3 = I + PC[a]	V + MR[c]	C14 = I + S
C4 = I + BD[c]	C9 = S + A[c]	C15 = V + I[c]
MR + PC[a,b]	DS + LN[e]	V + S[c]

Abbreviations: V = Vocabulary, S = Similarities, A = Arithmetic, DS = Digit Span, I = Information, C = Comprehension, LN = Letter–Number Sequencing, PC = Picture Completion, CD = Digit Symbol–Coding, BD = Block Design, MR = Matrix Reasoning, PA = Picture Arrangement, SS = Symbol Search.

Reliability and validity coefficients associated with each short-form combination are shown in Table O-6. See Exhibit 6-3 (page 138) for an explanation of the procedure used to obtain the estimated Deviation Quotients.

[a] This combination is useful for rapid screening.

[b] This combination is useful for hard-of-hearing examinees.

[c] This combination is one of the 10 best dyads.

[d] This combination is useful for rapid screening and is one of the 10 best dyads.

[e] This combination provides an estimate of the Working Memory factor.

[f] This combination provides an estimate of the Processing Speed factor.

Table O-8
Estimated WAIS–III Full Scale Deviation Quotients for Sum of Scaled Scores for Ten Best Short-Form Triads and Other Combinations

Sum of scaled scores	Combination																
	C2	C3	C4	C5	C6	C7	C8	C9	C10	C11	C12	C13	C14	C15	C16	C17	C18
3	43	43	43	44	45	45	45	46	47	47	47	47	47	48	48	48	51
4	45	45	45	46	47	47	47	48	49	49	49	49	49	49	50	50	52
5	47	47	47	48	49	49	49	50	51	51	51	51	51	51	52	52	54
6	49	49	49	50	51	51	51	52	53	53	53	53	53	53	54	54	56
7	51	51	52	52	53	53	53	54	55	55	55	55	55	55	56	56	58
8	53	54	54	54	55	55	55	56	57	57	57	57	57	57	57	57	60
9	55	56	56	56	57	57	57	58	59	59	59	59	59	59	59	59	62
10	58	58	58	59	59	59	59	60	61	61	61	61	61	61	61	61	63
11	60	60	60	61	61	61	61	62	63	63	63	63	63	63	63	63	65
12	62	62	62	63	63	63	63	64	65	65	65	65	65	65	65	65	67
13	64	64	64	65	65	65	65	66	67	67	67	67	67	67	67	67	69
14	66	66	66	67	67	67	67	68	68	69	69	69	69	69	69	69	71
15	68	68	68	69	69	69	69	70	70	71	71	71	71	71	71	71	73
16	70	70	71	71	71	71	71	72	72	73	73	73	73	73	73	73	74
17	72	73	73	73	73	73	73	74	74	74	75	75	75	75	75	75	76
18	75	75	75	75	75	75	76	76	76	76	76	77	77	77	77	77	78
19	77	77	77	77	77	78	78	78	78	78	78	78	79	79	79	79	80
20	79	79	79	79	79	80	80	80	80	80	80	80	80	81	81	81	82
21	81	81	81	81	82	82	82	82	82	82	82	82	82	83	83	83	84
22	83	83	83	83	84	84	84	84	84	84	84	84	84	84	85	85	85
23	85	85	85	85	86	86	86	86	86	86	86	86	86	86	86	86	87
24	87	87	87	88	88	88	88	88	88	88	88	88	88	88	88	88	89
25	89	89	89	90	90	90	90	90	90	90	90	90	90	90	90	90	91
26	92	92	92	92	92	92	92	92	92	92	92	92	92	92	92	92	93
27	94	94	94	94	94	94	94	94	94	94	94	94	94	94	94	94	95
28	96	96	96	96	96	96	96	96	96	96	96	96	96	96	96	96	96
29	98	98	98	98	98	98	98	98	98	98	98	98	98	98	98	98	98
30	100	100	100	100	100	100	100	100	100	100	100	100	100	100	100	100	100
31	102	102	102	102	102	102	102	102	102	102	102	102	102	102	102	102	102
32	104	104	104	104	104	104	104	104	104	104	104	104	104	104	104	104	104
33	106	106	106	106	106	106	106	106	106	106	106	106	106	106	106	106	105
34	108	108	108	108	108	108	108	108	108	108	108	108	108	108	108	108	107
35	111	111	111	110	110	110	110	110	110	110	110	110	110	110	110	110	109
36	113	113	113	112	112	112	112	112	112	112	112	112	112	112	112	112	111
37	115	115	115	115	114	114	114	114	114	114	114	114	114	114	114	114	113
38	117	117	117	117	116	116	116	116	116	116	116	116	116	116	115	115	115
39	119	119	119	119	118	118	118	118	118	118	118	118	118	118	117	117	117	116
40	121	121	121	121	121	120	120	120	120	120	120	120	120	119	119	119	118
41	123	123	123	123	123	122	122	122	122	122	122	122	121	121	121	121	120
42	125	125	125	125	125	125	124	124	124	124	124	123	123	123	123	123	122
43	128	127	127	127	127	127	127	126	126	126	125	125	125	125	125	125	124
44	130	130	129	129	129	129	129	128	128	127	127	127	127	127	127	127	126
45	132	132	132	131	131	131	131	130	130	129	129	129	129	129	129	129	127
46	134	134	134	133	133	133	133	132	132	131	131	131	131	131	131	131	129
47	136	136	136	135	135	135	135	134	133	133	133	133	133	133	133	133	131
48	138	138	138	137	137	137	137	136	135	135	135	135	135	135	135	135	133
49	140	140	140	139	139	139	139	138	137	137	137	137	137	137	137	137	135

(Continued)

Table O-8 (*Continued*)

Sum of scaled scores	Combination																
	C2	C3	C4	C5	C6	C7	C8	C9	C10	C11	C12	C13	C14	C15	C16	C17	C18
50	142	142	142	141	141	141	141	140	139	139	139	139	139	139	139	139	137
51	145	144	144	144	143	143	143	142	141	141	141	141	141	141	141	141	138
52	147	146	146	146	145	145	145	144	143	143	143	143	143	143	143	143	140
53	149	149	148	148	147	147	147	146	145	145	145	145	145	145	144	144	142
54	151	151	151	150	149	149	149	148	147	147	147	147	147	147	146	146	144
55	153	153	153	152	151	151	151	150	149	149	149	149	149	149	148	148	146
56	155	155	155	154	153	153	153	152	151	151	151	151	151	151	150	150	148
57	157	157	157	156	155	155	155	154	153	153	153	153	153	152	152	152	149

Note. The subtest combinations in each column are as follows:

C2 = PC + CD + MR[a]
C3 = I + CD + MR[b]
C4 = PC + CD + BD[a]
C5 = PC + BD + MR[a]
C6 = CD + PC + MR[b]
     CD + A + PC[c]
C7 = A + I + PC[b]

C8 = I + S + DS
C9 = PC + BD + MR[b]
     V + A + BD[c]
     V + A + PA[c]
     A + DS + LN[d]
C10 = V + A + MR[c]
C11 = A + I + MR[b]

C12 = V + I + D[c]
C13 = S + I + MR[c]
C14 = V + S + BD[c]
C15 = V + C + MR[c]
C16 = V + I + MR[c]
C17 = V + S + MR[c]
C18 = V + S + I[e]

Abbreviations: V = Vocabulary, S = Similarities, A = Arithmetic, DS = Digit Span, I = Information, C = Comprehension, LN = Letter–Number Sequencing, PC = Picture Completion, CD = Digit Symbol—Coding, BD = Block Design, MR = Matrix Reasoning, PA = Picture Arrangement, SS = Symbol Search.

Reliability and validity coefficients associated with each short-form combination are shown in Table O-6. See Exhibit 6-3 (page 138) for an explanation of the procedure used to obtain the estimated Deviation Quotients.

[a] This combination is useful for rapid screening.

[b] This combination is useful for hard-of-hearing examinees. It also represents the subtests in the Perceptual Organization Index.

[c] This combination is one of the 10 best short-form triads.

[d] This combination represents the subtests in the Working Memory Index.

[e] This combination represents the subtests in the Verbal Comprehension Index.

Table 0-9
Estimated WAIS–III Full Scale Deviation Quotients for Sum of Scaled Scores for Ten Best Short-Form Tetrads and Other Combinations

Sum of scaled scores	Combination															
	C2	C3	C4	C5	C6	C7	C8	C9	C10	C11	C12	C13	C14	C15	C16	C17
4	41	41	42	42	42	43	43	43	44	44	44	44	45	45	46	46
5	42	43	44	44	44	44	45	45	45	45	46	46	46	47	47	48
6	44	44	45	45	46	46	46	47	47	47	47	48	48	48	49	49
7	46	46	47	47	47	48	48	48	48	48	49	49	49	50	50	51
8	47	48	48	49	49	49	50	50	50	50	50	51	51	51	52	52
9	49	49	50	50	50	51	51	51	51	51	52	52	52	53	53	54
10	50	51	52	52	52	52	53	53	53	53	54	54	54	54	55	55
11	52	53	53	53	54	54	54	54	55	55	55	55	55	56	56	57
12	54	54	55	55	55	56	56	56	56	56	57	57	57	57	58	58
13	55	56	56	57	57	57	57	58	58	58	58	58	58	59	59	60
14	57	58	58	58	58	59	59	59	59	59	60	60	60	61	61	61
15	59	59	60	60	60	60	61	61	61	61	61	61	62	62	62	63
16	60	61	61	61	62	62	62	62	62	62	63	63	63	64	64	64
17	62	62	63	63	63	63	64	64	64	64	64	65	65	65	65	66
18	64	64	64	65	65	65	65	65	65	66	66	66	66	67	67	67
19	65	66	66	66	66	67	67	67	67	67	68	68	68	68	68	69
20	67	67	68	68	68	68	68	69	69	69	69	69	69	70	70	70
21	69	69	69	69	70	70	70	70	70	70	71	71	71	71	71	72
22	70	71	71	71	71	71	72	72	72	72	72	72	72	73	73	73
23	72	72	73	73	73	73	73	73	73	73	74	74	74	74	74	75
24	74	74	74	74	74	75	75	75	75	75	75	75	75	76	76	76
25	75	76	76	76	76	76	76	76	76	77	77	77	77	77	77	78
26	77	77	77	78	78	78	78	78	78	78	78	78	78	79	79	79
27	79	79	79	79	79	79	80	80	80	80	80	80	80	80	80	81
28	80	80	81	81	81	81	81	81	81	81	81	81	82	82	82	82
29	82	82	82	82	82	83	83	83	83	83	83	83	83	83	83	84
30	83	84	84	84	84	84	84	84	84	84	85	85	85	85	85	85
31	85	85	85	86	86	86	86	86	86	86	86	86	86	86	86	87
32	87	87	87	87	87	87	87	87	87	87	88	88	88	88	88	88
33	88	89	89	89	89	89	89	89	89	89	89	89	89	89	89	90
34	90	90	90	90	90	90	91	91	91	91	91	91	91	91	91	91
35	92	92	92	92	92	92	92	92	92	92	92	92	92	92	92	93
36	93	93	94	94	94	94	94	94	94	94	94	94	94	94	94	94
37	95	95	95	95	95	95	95	95	95	95	95	95	95	95	95	96
38	97	97	97	97	97	97	97	97	97	97	97	97	97	97	97	97
39	98	98	98	98	98	98	98	98	98	98	98	98	98	98	98	99
40	100	100	100	100	100	100	100	100	100	100	100	100	100	100	100	100
41	102	102	102	102	102	102	102	102	102	102	102	102	102	102	102	101
42	103	103	103	103	103	103	103	103	103	103	103	103	103	103	103	103
43	105	105	105	105	105	105	105	105	105	105	105	105	105	105	105	104
44	107	107	106	106	106	106	106	106	106	106	106	106	106	106	106	106
45	108	108	108	108	108	108	108	108	108	108	108	108	108	108	108	107
46	110	110	110	110	110	110	109	109	109	109	109	109	109	109	109	109
47	112	111	111	111	111	111	111	111	111	111	111	111	111	111	111	110
48	113	113	113	113	113	113	113	113	113	113	112	112	112	112	112	112
49	115	115	115	114	114	114	114	114	114	114	114	114	114	114	114	113

(Continued)

Table O-9 (*Continued*)

Sum of scaled scores	Combination															
	C2	*C3*	*C4*	*C5*	*C6*	*C7*	*C8*	*C9*	*C10*	*C11*	*C12*	*C13*	*C14*	*C15*	*C16*	*C17*
50	117	116	116	116	116	116	116	116	116	116	115	115	115	115	115	115
51	118	118	118	118	118	117	117	117	117	117	117	117	117	117	117	116
52	120	120	119	119	119	119	119	119	119	119	119	119	118	118	118	118
53	121	121	121	121	121	121	120	120	120	120	120	120	120	120	120	119
54	123	123	123	122	122	122	122	122	122	122	122	122	122	121	123	121
55	125	124	124	124	124	124	124	124	124	123	123	123	123	123	124	122
56	126	126	126	126	126	125	125	125	125	125	125	125	125	124	126	124
57	128	128	127	127	127	127	127	127	127	127	126	126	126	126	127	125
58	130	129	129	129	129	129	128	128	128	128	128	128	128	127	129	127
59	131	131	131	131	130	130	130	130	130	130	129	129	129	129	130	128
60	133	133	132	132	132	132	132	131	131	131	131	131	131	130	132	130
61	135	134	134	134	134	133	133	133	133	133	132	132	132	132	133	131
62	136	136	136	135	135	135	135	135	135	134	134	134	134	133	135	133
63	138	138	137	137	137	137	136	136	136	136	136	135	135	135	136	134
64	140	139	139	139	138	138	138	138	138	138	137	137	137	136	138	136
65	141	141	140	140	140	140	139	139	139	139	139	139	138	138	139	137
66	143	142	142	142	142	141	141	141	141	141	140	140	140	139	141	139
67	145	144	144	143	143	143	143	142	142	142	142	142	142	141	142	140
68	146	146	145	145	145	144	144	144	144	144	143	143	143	143	144	142
69	148	147	147	147	146	146	146	146	145	145	145	145	145	144	145	143
70	150	149	148	148	148	148	147	147	147	147	146	146	146	146	147	145
71	151	151	150	150	150	149	149	149	149	149	148	148	148	147	148	146
72	153	152	152	151	151	151	150	150	150	150	150	149	149	149	150	148
73	154	154	153	153	153	152	152	152	152	152	151	151	151	150	151	149
74	156	156	155	155	154	154	154	153	153	153	153	152	152	152	153	151
75	158	157	156	156	156	156	155	155	155	155	154	154	154	153	154	152
76	159	159	158	158	158	157	157	157	156	156	156	156	155	155	156	154

Note. The subtest combinations in each column are as follows:

C2 = DS + I + PC + MR[a]
C3 = A + I + PC + CD[a]
C4 = PC + CD + BD + MR[b]
C5 = A + S + CD + LN
C6 = MR + PC + CD + SS
C7 = V + DS + I + BD[c]
      A + I + CD + MR[a]

C8 = I + A + PC + BD
C9 = V + A + PC + MR[c]
C10 = A + I + PC + MR[a]
C11 = V + A + BD + PA[c]
C12 = V + A + DS + S
C13 = V + I + PC + MR[c]

C14 = V + S + A + PC[c]
C15 = V + I + BD + MR[c]
       V + S + A + PA[c]
C16 = V + S + A + BD[c]
       V + A + I + BD[c]
C17 = V + S + A + MR[c]

Abbreviations: V = Vocabulary, S = Similarities, A = Arithmetic, DS = Digit Span, I = Information, C = Comprehension, LN = Letter–Number Sequencing, PC = Picture Completion, CD = Digit Symbol—Coding, BD = Block Design, MR = Matrix Reasoning, PA = Picture Arrangement, SS = Symbol Search.

Reliability and validity coefficients associated with each short-form combination are shown in Table O-6. See Exhibit 6-3 (page 138) for an explanation of the procedure used to obtain the estimated Deviation Quotients.

[a] This combination is useful for rapid screening.
[b] This combination is useful for hard-of-hearing examinees.
[c] This combination is one of the 10 best tetrads.

Table O-10
Estimated WAIS–III Full Scale Deviation Quotients for Sum of Scaled Scores for Ten Best Short-Form Pentads and Other Combinations

Sum of scaled scores	Combination										
	C2	C3	C4	C5	C6	C7	C8	C9	C10	C11	C12
5	38	39	41	41	41	42	43	43	43	44	44
6	40	40	42	42	43	43	45	45	45	45	45
7	41	42	43	43	44	45	46	46	46	46	46
8	42	43	45	45	45	46	47	47	47	47	48
9	44	44	46	46	46	47	48	48	48	49	49
10	45	46	47	47	48	49	50	50	50	50	50
11	46	47	49	49	49	50	51	51	51	51	51
12	48	48	50	50	50	51	52	52	52	52	53
13	49	50	51	51	52	52	53	53	54	54	54
14	51	51	52	53	53	54	55	55	55	55	55
15	52	52	54	54	54	55	56	56	56	56	56
16	53	54	55	55	56	56	57	57	57	57	58
17	55	55	56	57	57	58	58	59	59	59	59
18	56	57	58	58	58	59	60	60	60	60	60
19	57	58	59	59	59	60	61	61	61	61	61
20	59	59	60	61	61	61	62	62	62	62	63
21	60	61	62	62	62	63	63	64	64	64	64
22	62	62	63	63	63	64	65	65	65	65	65
23	63	63	64	64	65	65	66	66	66	66	66
24	64	65	66	66	66	67	67	67	67	67	68
25	66	66	67	67	67	68	68	69	69	69	69
26	67	67	68	68	69	69	70	70	70	70	70
27	68	69	70	70	70	70	71	71	71	71	71
28	70	70	71	71	71	72	72	72	72	72	73
29	71	71	72	72	73	73	74	74	74	74	74
30	73	73	74	74	74	74	75	75	75	75	75
31	74	74	75	75	75	76	76	76	76	76	76
32	75	76	76	76	76	77	77	77	77	77	78
33	77	77	78	78	78	78	79	79	79	79	79
34	78	78	79	79	79	79	80	80	80	80	80
35	79	80	80	80	80	81	81	81	81	81	81
36	81	81	82	82	82	82	82	82	82	82	83
37	82	82	83	83	83	83	84	84	84	84	84
38	84	84	84	84	84	85	85	85	85	85	85
39	85	85	85	86	86	86	86	86	86	86	86
40	86	86	87	87	87	87	87	87	87	87	88
41	88	88	88	88	88	88	89	89	89	89	89
42	89	89	89	89	90	90	90	90	90	90	90
43	90	90	91	91	91	91	91	91	91	91	91
44	92	92	92	92	92	92	92	92	92	92	93
45	93	93	93	93	93	94	94	94	94	94	94
46	95	95	95	95	95	95	95	95	95	95	95
47	96	96	96	96	96	96	96	96	96	96	96
48	97	97	97	97	97	97	97	97	97	97	98
49	99	99	99	99	99	99	99	99	99	99	99
50	100	100	100	100	100	100	100	100	100	100	100
51	101	101	101	101	101	101	101	101	101	101	101
52	103	103	103	103	103	103	103	103	103	103	102
53	104	104	104	104	104	104	104	104	104	104	104
54	105	105	105	105	105	105	105	105	105	105	105

(Continued)

Table O-10 (*Continued*)

Sum of scaled scores	Combination										
	C2	C3	C4	C5	C6	C7	C8	C9	C10	C11	C12
55	107	107	107	107	107	106	106	106	106	106	106
56	108	108	108	108	108	108	108	108	108	108	107
57	110	110	109	109	109	109	109	109	109	109	109
58	111	111	111	111	110	110	110	110	110	110	110
59	112	112	112	112	112	112	111	111	111	111	111
60	114	114	113	113	113	113	113	113	113	113	112
61	115	115	115	114	114	114	114	114	114	114	114
62	116	116	116	116	116	115	115	115	115	115	115
63	118	118	117	117	117	117	116	116	116	116	116
64	119	119	118	118	118	118	118	118	118	118	117
65	121	120	120	120	120	119	119	119	119	119	119
66	122	122	121	121	121	121	120	120	120	120	120
67	123	123	122	122	122	122	121	121	121	121	121
68	125	124	124	124	124	123	123	123	123	123	122
69	126	126	125	125	125	124	124	124	124	124	124
70	127	127	126	126	126	126	125	125	125	125	125
71	129	129	128	128	127	127	126	126	126	126	126
72	130	130	129	129	129	128	128	128	128	128	127
73	132	131	130	130	130	130	129	129	129	129	129
74	133	133	132	132	131	131	130	130	130	130	130
75	134	134	133	133	133	132	132	131	131	131	131
76	136	135	134	134	134	133	133	133	133	133	132
77	137	137	136	136	135	135	134	134	134	134	134
78	138	138	137	137	137	136	135	135	135	135	135
79	140	139	138	138	138	137	137	136	136	136	136
80	141	141	140	139	139	139	138	138	138	138	137
81	143	142	141	141	141	140	139	139	139	139	139
82	144	143	142	142	142	141	140	140	140	140	140
83	145	145	144	143	143	142	142	141	141	141	141
84	147	146	145	145	144	144	143	143	143	143	142
85	148	148	146	146	146	145	144	144	144	144	144
86	149	149	148	147	147	146	145	145	145	145	145
87	151	150	149	149	148	148	147	147	146	146	146
88	152	152	150	150	150	149	148	148	148	148	147
89	154	153	151	151	151	150	149	149	149	149	149
90	155	154	153	153	152	151	150	150	150	150	150
91	156	156	154	154	154	153	152	152	152	151	151
92	158	157	155	155	155	154	153	153	153	153	152
93	159	158	157	157	156	155	154	154	154	154	154
94	160	160	158	158	157	157	155	155	155	155	155

Note. The subtest combinations in each column are as follows:

C2 = DS + I + PC + CD + MR[a]	C7 = V + I + CD + BD + MR[b]	C10 = V + S + A + PC + MR[b]
C3 = A + DS + I + PC + CD[a]	V + DS + I + BD + MR[b]	C11 = V + A + I + PC + MR[b]
C4 = A + I + PC + CD + MR[a]	C8 = V + A + C + PC + MR[b]	V + S + A + BD + PA[b]
C5 = A + DS + I + PC + MR[a]	V + A + I + PC + BD[b]	C12 = V + A + I + BD + PA[b]
C6 = V + DS + I + PC + MR[b]	C9 = V + A + C + BD + PA[b]	

Abbreviations: V = Vocabulary, S = Similarities, A = Arithmetic, DS = Digit Span, I = Information, C = Comprehension, LN = Letter–Number Sequencing, PC = Picture Completion, CD = Digit Symbol—Coding, BD = Block Design, MR = Matrix Reasoning, PA = Picture Arrangement, SS = Symbol Search.

Reliability and validity coefficients associated with each short-form combination are shown in Table O-6. See Exhibit 6-3 (page 138) for an explanation of the procedure used to obtain the estimated Deviation Quotients.

[a] This combination is useful for a rapid screening.
[b] This combination is one of the 10 best pentads.

Table O-11
Estimated WAIS–III Full Scale Deviation Quotients for Sum of Scaled Scores for One Six-Subtest Short-Form Combination and Two Seven-Subtest Short-Form Combinations

Sum of scaled scores	Combination			Sum of scaled scores	Combination			Sum of scaled scores	Combination		
	C2	C3	C4		C2	C3	C4		C2	C3	C4
6	43	—	—					105	147	134	134
7	44	39	39	56	96	86	86	106	148	135	135
8	45	40	40	57	97	87	87	107	149	136	136
9	46	41	41	58	98	88	88	108	150	137	137
10	48	42	42	59	99	89	89	109	151	138	138
11	49	42	43	60	100	90	90	110	152	139	139
12	50	43	44	61	101	91	91	111	154	140	140
13	51	44	45	62	102	92	92	112	155	141	141
14	52	45	46	63	103	93	93	113	156	142	142
15	53	46	47	64	104	94	94	114	157	143	143
16	54	47	48	65	105	95	95	115	158	144	144
17	55	48	49	66	106	96	96	116		145	145
18	56	49	50	67	107	97	97	117		146	146
19	57	50	51	68	108	98	98	118		147	147
20	58	51	51	69	109	99	99	119		148	148
21	59	52	52	70	110	100	100	120		149	149
22	60	53	53	71	112	101	101	121		150	149
23	61	54	54	72	113	102	102	122		151	150
24	62	55	55	73	114	103	103	123		152	151
25	63	56	56	74	115	104	104	124		153	152
26	64	57	57	75	116	105	105	125		154	153
27	65	58	58	76	117	106	106	126		155	154
28	66	59	59	77	118	107	107	127		156	155
29	67	60	60	78	119	108	108	128		157	156
30	69	61	61	79	120	109	109	129		158	157
31	70	62	62	80	121	110	110	130		158	158
32	71	63	63	81	122	111	111	131		159	159
33	72	64	64	82	123	112	112	132		160	160
34	73	65	65	83	124	113	113	133		161	161
35	74	66	66	84	125	114	114	134			
36	75	67	67	85	126	115	115	135			
37	76	68	68	86	127	116	116	136			
38	77	69	69	87	128	117	116	137			
39	78	70	70	88	129	118	117	138			
40	79	71	71	89	130	119	118	139			
41	80	72	72	90	131	119	119	140			
42	81	73	73	91	133	120	120	141			
43	82	74	74	92	134	121	121	142			
44	83	75	75	93	135	122	122	143			
45	84	76	76	94	136	123	123	144			
46	85	77	77	95	137	124	124	145			
47	86	78	78	96	138	125	125	146			
48	87	79	79	97	139	126	126	147			
49	88	80	80	98	140	127	127	148			
50	90	81	81	99	141	128	128	149			
51	91	81	82	100	142	129	129	150			
52	92	82	83	101	143	130	130	151			
53	93	83	84	102	144	131	131	152			
54	94	84	84	103	145	132	132				
55	95	85	85	104	146	133	133				

(*Continued*)

Table O-11 (*Continued*)

Note. The subtest combinations in each column are as follows:

C2 = V + S + I + PC + BD + MR[a]
C3 = I + A + DS + S + PC + BD + CD[b]
C4 = I + A + DS + S + PC + MR +CD[c]

Abbreviations: V = Vocabulary, S = Similarities, A = Arithmetic, DS = Digit Span, I = Information,
PC = Picture Completion, CD = Digit Symbol—Coding, BD = Block Design, MR = Matrix Reasoning.
Reliability and validity coefficients associated with each short-form combination are shown in Table O-6.
See Exhibit 6-3 (page 138) for an explanation of the procedure used to obtain the estimated Deviation Quotients.
[a] The reliability and validity of this combination are r_{xx} = .966 and r = .946, respectively.
[b] The reliability and validity of this combination are r_{xx} = .965 and r = .942, respectively.
[c] The reliability and validity of this combination are r_{xx} = .967 and r = .944, respectively.

REFERENCES

Albert, M. L., Goodglass, H., Helm, N. A., Rubens, A. B., & Alexander, M. P. (1981). *Clinical aspects of dysphasia.* New York: Springer-Verlag.

Axelrod, B. N., Woodard, J. L., Schretlen, D., & Benedict, R. H. B. (1996). Corrected estimates of WAIS–R short form reliability and standard errors of measurement. *Psychological Assessment, 8,* 222–223.

Baddley, A. (1990). *Human memory: Theory and practice.* Boston: Allyn & Bacon.

Evans, R. G. (1985). Accuracy of the Satz-Mogel procedure in estimating WAIS–R IQs that are in the normal range. *Journal of Clinical Psychology, 41,* 100–103.

Flynn, J. R. (1984). The mean IQ of Americans: Massive gains 1932 to 1978. *Psychological Bulletin, 95,* 29–51.

Flynn, J. R. (1987). Massive IQ gains in 14 nations: What IQ tests really measure. *Psychological Bulletin, 101,* 171–191.

Kaplan, E., Fein, D., Morris, R., & Delis, D. C. (1991). *WAIS–R as a neuropsychological instrument.* San Antonio, TX: The Psychological Corporation.

Kaufman, A. S. (1990). *Assessing adolescent and adult intelligence.* Boston: Allyn & Bacon.

Matarazzo, J. D., Daniel, M. H., Prifitera, A., & Herman, D. O. (1988). Inter-subtest scatter in the WAIS–R standardization sample. *Journal of Clinical Psychology, 44,* 940–950.

Mattis, P. J., Hanny, H. J., & Meyers, C. A. (1992). Efficacy of the Satz-Mogel short form WAIS–R for tumor patients with lateralized lesions. *Psychological Assessment, 4,* 357–362.

McArdel, J. M., Prescott, C. A., Hamagami, F., & Horn, J. L. (1998). A contemporary method for developmental-genetic analyses of age changes in intellectual abilities. *Developmental Neuropsychology, 14,* 69–114.

Paolo, A. M., & Ryan, J. J. (1992). WAIS–R abbreviated forms in the elderly: A comparison of the Satz-Mogel with a seven-subtest short form. *Psychological Assessment, 5,* 425–429.

Paolo, A. M., & Ryan, J. J. (1993). Test-retest stability of the Satz-Mogel WAIS–R short form in a sample of normal persons 75 to 87 of age. *Archives of Clinical Neuropsychology, 8,* 397–404.

Paolo, A. M., Ryan, J. J., Ward, L. C., & Hilmer, C. D. (1996). Different WAIS–R short forms and their relation to ethnicity. *Personality and Individual Differences, 21,* 851–856.

The Psychological Corporation. (1992). *The Wechsler Individual Achievement Test.* San Antonio, TX: Author.

The Psychological Corporation. (1997). *WAIS–III—WMS–III Technical Manual.* San Antonio, TX: Author.

Ryan, J. J., Abraham, E., Axelrod, B. N., & Paolo, A. M. (1996). WAIS–R Verbal-Performance IQ discrepancies in persons with lateralized lesions: Utility of a seven-subtest short form. *Archives of Clinical Neuropsychology, 11,* 207–213.

Ryan, J. J., Lopez, S. J., & Sattler, J. M. (1998). *Age effects on Wechsler Adult Intelligence Scale–III subtests.* Unpublished manuscript.

Ryan, J. J., Paolo, A. M., & Brungardt, T. M. (1992). WAIS–R test-retest stability in normal persons 75 years and older. *The Clinical Neuropsychologist, 6,* 3–8.

Ryan, J. J., & Rosenberg, S. J. (1984). Administration time estimates for WAIS–R subtests and short forms in a clinical sample. *Journal of Psychoeducational Assessment, 2,* 125–129.

Ryan, J. J., Werth, T., & Lopez, S. J. (1998). *Administration time estimates for WAIS–III subtests, scales, and short forms in a clinical sample.* Unpublished manuscript.

Sattler, J. M., & Ryan, J. J. (1998). *Comparison of two methods of computing short-form Deviation Quotients on the WAIS–III.* Unpublished manuscript.

Satz, P., & Mogel, S. (1962). An abbreviation of the WAIS for clinical use. *Journal of Clinical Psychology, 18,* 77–79.

Shindell, S. (1989). Assessing the visually impaired older adult. In T. Hunt & C. J. Lindley (Eds.), *Testing older adults.* Austin, TX: Pro-Ed.

Silverstein, A. B. (1982). Validity of Satz-Mogel-Yudin-type short forms. *Journal of Consulting and Clinical Psychology, 50,* 20–21.

Silverstein, A. B. (1990a). Notes on the reliability of Wechsler short forms. *Journal of Clinical Psychology, 46,* 194–196.

Silverstein, A. B. (1990b). Short forms of individual intelligence tests. *Psychological Assessment: A*

Journal of Consulting and Clinical Psychology, 2, 3–11.

Tellegen, A., & Briggs, P. F. (1967). Old wine in new skins: Grouping Wechsler subtests into new scales. *Journal of Consulting Psychology, 31*, 499–506.

Thorndike, R. L., Hagen, E. P., & Sattler, J. M. (1986). *Guide for administering and scoring the Stanford-Binet Intelligence Scale: Fourth Edition*. Chicago: Riverside Publishing.

Ward, L. C. (1990). Prediction of Verbal, Performance, and Full Scale IQs from seven sub-tests of the WAIS–R. *Journal of Clinical Psychology, 46*, 436–440.

Wechsler, D. (1939). *Wechsler-Bellevue Intelligence Scale*. New York: The Psychological Corporation.

Wechsler, D. (1981). *Wechsler Adult Intelligence Scale–Revised*. San Antonio, TX: The Psychological Corporation.

Wechsler, D. (1997). *WAIS–III Administration and Scoring Manual*. San Antonio, TX: The Psychological Corporation.

INDEX

Abraham, E., 1242
Albert, M. L., 1227
Alexander, M. P., 1227
Arithmetic, 1204, 1207, 1208, 1210, 1214–1222, 1224, 1230, 1236–1242, 1244, 1245, 1247, 1250, 1255, 1257, 1258, 1261, 1263
Atkinson, L., 1241, 1242
Axelrod, B. N., 1242

Baddley, A., 1247
Benedict, R. H. B., 1242
Block Design, 1204, 1207, 1208, 1210, 1213– 1222, 1224, 1230, 1235, 1237–1239, 1241, 1242, 1248–1250, 1252, 1258, 1259, 1261, 1263
Briggs, P. F., 1206, 1227, 1239, 1240, 1261, 1262
Brungardt, T. M., 1208

Comprehension, 1204, 1207, 1208, 1210, 1213–1224, 1232, 1236–1238, 1242, 1243, 1246, 1255, 1257–1261, 1263

Daniel, M. H., 1256
Delis, D. C., 1236
Digit Span, 1204, 1205, 1207, 1208, 1210, 1213–1222, 1224–1227, 1231, 1235–1240, 1242, 1244, 1245, 1247, 1254, 1255, 1257, 1258, 1261, 1263
Digit Symbol—Coding, 1204–1208, 1210, 1213–1226, 1229, 1236–1240, 1242, 1248, 1249, 1251, 1252, 1255, 1258, 1260, 1261, 1263
Digit Symbol—Copy, 1222, 1223, 1229, 1234, 1248, 1249
Digit Symbol—Incidental Learning, 1222, 1223, 1229, 1248, 1249

Evans, R. G., 1240, 1241

Factor analyses, 1214–1219
Fein, D., 1236
Flynn, J. R., 1212

g measure, 1213, 1215, 1217, 1218, 1223, 1240, 1241, 1243–1252, 1263
Goodglass, H., 1227

Hagen, E. P., 1212
Hamagami, F., 1259
Hanny, H. J., 1241
Helm, N. A., 1227
Herman, D. O., 1256
Hilmer, C. D., 1242
Horn, J. L., 1259

Information, 1204, 1207, 1208, 1210, 1213–1219, 1221–1224, 1231, 1236–1239, 1241–1246, 1251, 1257, 1258, 1260, 1261, 1263

Kaplan, E., 1236
Kaufman, A. S., 1257

Letter–Number Sequencing, 1204–1208, 1210, 1213–1215, 1217, 1218, 1220, 1222, 1224–1226, 1233, 1237–1240, 1245–1247, 1254, 1255, 1257, 1258, 1260–1263
Lopez, S. J., 1239, 1257

Matarazzo, J. D., 1256
Matrix Reasoning, 1204–1210, 1214–1219, 1221, 1223, 1224, 1231, 1237–1239, 1241, 1242, 1249, 1250, 1252, 1258, 1259, 1261, 1263
Mattis, P. J., 1241
McArdle, J. M., 1259
Meyers, C. A., 1241
Mogel, S., 1240, 1241
Morris, R., 1236

Object Assembly, 1204–1208, 1210, 1213–1222, 1224, 1226, 1233, 1237, 1238, 1248, 1250, 1252, 1254, 1258, 1259, 1263

Paolo, A. M., 1208, 1241, 1242

Perceptual Organization, 1207–1210, 1214–1218, 1220, 1222, 1223, 1234, 1240, 1242, 1248–1252, 1255, 1256, 1259, 1261, 1263
Picture Arrangement, 1204, 1207, 1208, 1210, 1212, 1214–1222, 1226, 1232, 1236, 1237, 1251, 1255, 1258, 1260, 1261, 1263
Picture Completion, 1204, 1207–1211, 1213–1219, 1221–1225, 1228, 1236–1239, 1241, 1242, 1247, 1248, 1254, 1258, 1261, 1263, 1264
Prescott, C. A., 1259
Prifitera, A., 1256
Processing Speed, 1207–1210, 1214, 1215, 1217, 1218, 1220, 1223, 1234, 1249, 1251, 1252, 1255, 1256, 1259, 1261–1263
Psychological Corporation, The, 1205, 1207–1215, 1238, 1240, 1247, 1249, 1253, 1260

Rosenberg S. J., 1242
Rubens, A. B., 1227
Ryan, J. J., 1208, 1215, 1239–1242, 1257

Sattler, J. M., 1212, 1215, 1240, 1257
Satz, P., 1240, 1241
Schretlen, D., 1242
Shindell, S., 1236
Short forms of WAIS–III, 1239–1242
Silverstein, A. B., 1239–1241
Similarities, 1204, 1207, 1208, 1210, 1213–1224, 1229, 1237, 1238, 1241–1244, 1246, 1257–1261, 1263
Standard Progressive Matrices, 1211, 1213
Stanford-Binet Intelligence Scale: Fourth Edition, 1211–1213
Symbol Search, 1204–1208, 1210, 1213–1226, 1232, 1235–1240, 1249, 1251, 1252, 1254, 1255, 1257, 1258, 1260–1263

Tellegen, A., 1206, 1227, 1239, 1240, 1262

Thinking through the issues, 1260
Thorndike, R. L., 1212
Tulsky, D., 1238, 1240, 1247, 1249, 1253

Verbal Comprehension, 1207–1210, 1214–1218, 1220, 1222, 1223, 1234, 1240, 1242, 1243, 1246, 1251, 1255, 1256, 1259, 1261, 1263
Vocabulary, 1204, 1206, 1207, 1208, 1210–1219, 1221–1224, 1228, 1237–1239, 1241, 1243, 1244, 1246, 1251, 1254, 1255, 1257–1263

Ward, L. C., 1242
Wechsler Adult Intelligence Scale–Revised (WAIS–R) 1203, 1204, 1208, 1210–1213, 1221–1224, 1240, 1242, 1258, 1259, 1261, 1262
Wechsler Adult Intelligence Scale–Third Edition (WAIS–III). *See also individual subtests*
administration, 1222, 1225–1239
administrative checklist, 1228–1235
age and subtest performance, 1257–1259
assets, 1259, 1260
auditory functions, 1225
basal level, 1225, 1238, 1239
ceiling level, 1225
comparison with WAIS–R, 1221, 1222
comparison with WISC–III, 1242

concurrent validity, 1211–1213
confidence intervals, 1209, 1210
construct validity, 1213
content validity, 1211
convergent validity, 1213
Deviation IQs, 1205, 1206
discontinuance-point scoring rule, 1238
discriminant validity, 1213
factor analyses, 1214–1219
g measure 1213, 1215, 1217, 1218, 1224, 1240, 1241, 1243–1252, 1263
highlights of changes, 1223, 1224
Index scores, 1218, 1220
intercorrelations between subtests and scales, 1213, 1214
interpretation, 1252–1259
language functions, 1227, 1235
limitations, 1260
modifying standard procedures, 1238
motor functions, 1236
multiple comparisons, 1255
physical abilities, 1225, 1227, 1235, 1236
probing questions, 1238
profile analysis, 1252–1256
prorating procedure, 1206
range of Full Scale IQs, 1220, 1221
range of subtest scores, 1220
reliability, 1206–1210
repetition of items, 1238
Satz-Mogel abbreviated procedure, 1240, 1241
scaled scores, 1205, 1206
short forms, 1239–1242

spoiled responses, 1238
standard errors of measurement, 1206, 1207
standardization, 1204
starting-point scoring rule, 1227
statistically reliable vs. empirically observed IQ differences, 1256, 1257
study questions, 1263, 1264
subtest sequence, 1236, 1237
subtest specificity, 1217, 1218
test-retest stability, 1207–1209
validity, 1210–1213
visual functions, 1235, 1236
Wechsler-Bellevue Intelligence Scale, Form I, 1204
Wechsler, D., 1204, 1205, 1238, 1239
Wechsler Individual Achievement (WIAT), 1204, 1213, 1260
Wechsler Intelligence Scale for Children–Third Edition (WISC–III), 1204, 1205, 1211, 1212, 1213, 1222, 1225, 1242–1252, 1262
Wechsler Memory Scale-Third Edition (WMS–III), 1204, 1213, 1260
Wechsler Preschool and Primary Scale of Intelligence–Revised (WPPSI–R), 1204, 1205
Werth, T., 1240
Woodard, J. L., 1243
Working Memory, 1207–1210, 1213–1218, 1220, 1222, 1223, 1234, 1244–1247, 1250, 1252, 1255, 1256, 1259, 1261–1263